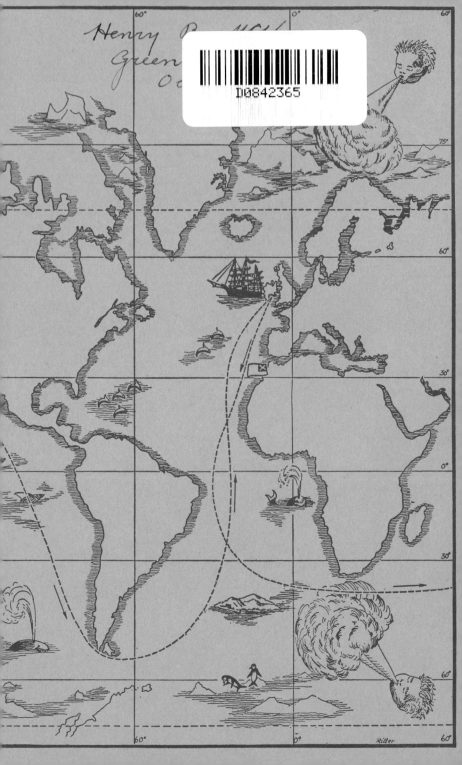

MANU FORTI

Henry Bacon McKoy
GREENVILLE, S. C.

GALLANT REBEL

GALLANT REBEL

THE FABULOUS CRUISE OF THE

C.S.S. *SHENANDOAH*

by

STANLEY F. HORN

———

New Brunswick

RUTGERS UNIVERSITY PRESS

1947

To B. W. H.

AUTHOR'S FOREWORD

IN ALL THE ANNALS of the men who go down to the sea in ships, there is not a more thrilling story than that of the Confederate cruiser *Shenandoah* (successor to the *Alabama*) which ravaged the United States merchant marine during the latter days of the War Between the States. Indeed, the depredations of the *Shenandoah* continued for several months after the war was (unknown to her commander) over. Far away in the North Pacific, Bering Sea, and Arctic Ocean, relentlessly destroying the New England whaling fleet in those waters, the commander of the Confederate cruiser knew nothing of the collapse of his government until he got the news by chance in the late summer of 1865. From his position in mid-Pacific he then took his ship to Liverpool, successfully eluding the United States warships sent out to intercept him, and on November 7th, 1865, flying the Confederate flag, sailed into Liverpool and surrendered to the British government.

The epic story of this around-the-world cruise of the last of the Confederate raiders has long remained buried in the dusty files of the Navy Department and in the scattered diaries and fugitive narratives of her officers. From these various sources the story has been pieced together and is here presented as an authentic historical narrative.

Author's Foreword

Assurance is given to the reader that every statement herein made is of unimpeachable historical accuracy, and every episode recounted had its counterpart in actual life. Some of the officers' diaries and stories fortunately preserved a wealth of detail and local color, from which it has been possible to capture the vivid feeling of this remarkable voyage.

Acknowledgment is made to the officials of the Navy Department in Washington who so kindly made available to me the log and other official documents relative to the *Shenandoah's* cruise, also to all others who helped me search out the details of the various phases of the expedition. I am especially indebted to the Confederate Museum at Richmond, Virginia, who permitted the use of the diaries of the cruiser's chief surgeon, Dr. Lining, and of Midshipman Mason.

The Author

CONTENTS

GALLANT REBEL

CHAPTER ONE

CONFEDERATE UNDERCOVER

MEN

————

AT ELEVEN O'CLOCK on the morning of October 7, 1864, Lieutenant William C. Whittle, Jr., of the Confederate States Navy, sat at a table in the coffeeroom of Wood's Hotel in London. Dressed in civilian clothes, he absently turned the pages of the morning *Times* which he held loosely in his strong, sunburnt hands. It was easy to see that the young man's attention was not fixed on the newspaper. At frequent intervals he pulled from his pocket his heavy gold watch, looked at it, and snapped it shut with a click. Between these consultations of his timepiece he kept his sharp, gray eyes on the door which separated the quiet coffeeroom from the clattering traffic noises of High Holborn outside, and on his weather-beaten, smooth-shaven young face there was the suggestion of a frown.

Lieutenant Whittle was feeling a little nervous, and just a little foolish and melodramatic as his glance dropped to the silk handkerchief which he had drawn through one of the buttonholes of his coat. He

3

scowled as he thought how absurd it was for a commissioned officer in the Confederate States Navy, a graduate of the Naval Academy at Annapolis, to be sitting in this unfamiliar little hotel in a bystreet of London waiting like a conspirator in some shilling-shocker novel for a mysterious stranger to come up and ask him if his name was Brown.

In obedience to his instructions, Brown was the name under which he had registered upon his arrival the night before. "W. C. Brown, Liverpool" he had scrawled in the book; and while he was doing it, even though he knew that London was infested with Yankee spies, he had not been able to repress a feeling that resort to such subterfuge was a foolish excess of caution. Why couldn't Bulloch have arranged some simpler and less theatrical means of giving him his orders? He knew that he had been sent to London as the first step in some new Confederate naval expedition, the exact nature of which was a carefully guarded secret for the present, but why couldn't his final instructions be given to him simply and directly without all this byplay?

Bulloch's letter, however, delivered to him the preceding day in London, had been unmistakably clear: "It has been arranged for you to be in the coffee-room of Wood's Hotel in London at 11 A.M. precisely tomorrow, and that you will sit in a prominent position, with a white pocket-handkerchief rove through a buttonhole of your coat, and a newspaper in your hand. In that attitude you will be recognized by our agent, who will call at the appointed time and ask if your name is Brown. You will . . ."

"Ah! If it isn't my old friend, Brown!" A hearty voice ended Lieutenant Whittle's ruminations, and he looked up to see a smiling, ruddy-faced man approaching with outstretched hand as though greeting an old acquaintance. Quickly Whittle rose to his feet, a tall, lean, lithe young man, with a shock of black hair brushed back sharply from the high forehead which stood out in pale contrast with his bronzed face.

"It's good to see you again," Whittle said. "Won't you sit down? Or, better still, let's go up to my room and have a cheroot. There's lots to talk about since the last time I saw you."

Arm in arm, they left the low-ceiled coffeeroom and mounted the creaking oak stairway—two old cronies meeting quite by chance in a public place and taking advantage of the opportunity to talk over old times together.

Once in Whittle's room, the door closed and locked, the ruddy face beamed on him approvingly.

"Capital!" the stranger exclaimed. "You carried that off nicely, Mr. Whittle—like an old-timer in the secret service. I don't think we were watched, but, if we were, I don't believe anybody would have suspected anything wrong."

Whittle, however, secure in the privacy of his own room, threw off the air of heartiness he had displayed in the coffeeroom.

"I might as well tell you right now," he said stiffly, "that I have no patience with all this flubdubbery. My own opinion is that Mr. Bulloch has been reading too many novels. What's the sense in all this round-

5

about nonsense in giving a naval officer his sailing orders? It's childish!" Lieutenant Whittle, at the mature age of twenty-four, had put away childish things.

"Maybe you think we take too many precautions," said the ruddy-faced man with an indulgent smile, "but you wouldn't feel that way if you'd had any experience with the Yankee spies in London. Why, man, the whole town is simply alive with them. The fellow who drives your cab or who waits on you at the table may be in the employ of that cunning devil Adams. I tell you, every move we make is watched. You'd hardly believe the pains I took to avoid being followed here."

Whittle laughed scornfully. "Nerves, just nerves," he said lightly.

"You just don't know," his visitor insisted patiently. "Let me remind you that Great Britain is a neutral. She's just a looker-on in this war between the North and the South. She has neutrality laws, and the Queen's officers are determined to enforce them. And even if the officers were inclined to wink at infractions, the Yankee busybodies wouldn't let them. They get their noses into everything. They watch us like hawks. They're smart, and they never sleep. They've upset our plans more than once, and we know that we can't be too careful, even if it does seem overcautious to you." He lowered his tone impressively. "We're playing for big stakes this time!"

"All right, all right," agreed Whittle petulantly. "Have it your own way. I'll get a false beard and wear it if you say so. But let's get down to business.

Here's my letter of introduction from Mr. Bulloch. He said you would have some instructions for me."

The ruddy-faced man took the letter and glanced at it casually, then looked Whittle steadily in the eye.

"The British merchant vessel, Sea King," he began, as though reciting a memorized piece, "lies in her berth at the East India docks, ballasted with coal. She clears early in the morning for Bombay and the China Sea. Her papers show her supercargo to be Mr. W. C. Forrester. You will be sailing on the Sea King when she leaves in the morning. Don't worry about your disinclination to go to Bombay. She may decide not to go there. And as for Mr. Forrester, permit me to make you known to him—you are Mr. Forrester, the supercargo of the Sea King! But perhaps I'd better explain."

"Yes, by all means do," said Whittle drily. "The plot is getting a trifle intricate for me."

It was in England that the principal working headquarters of the Confederate States Navy was maintained during the War Between the States. To be sure, the Secretary of the Navy, Mr. Mallory, had his office in Richmond, but during the early days of the war all the ports of the Southern States had been blockaded, and it was an effective blockade too, except for the dashes of the swift runners which slipped by the watch-dog fleets on dark nights when the moon was right.

In such circumstances, there was little chance for Confederate war vessels to operate out of home ports. Before the blockade Admiral Raphael Semmes had

7

been able to take the Sumter out of New Orleans, and a few other small warships had been fitted out in Confederate ports during those early days. It was in England, however, that the Confederacy's outstanding naval vessels were clandestinely built; and it was to the shipyards on the Mersey and the Clyde that Southern officials looked hopefully when their own ports were bottled up tightly.

The Confederates were fortunate in having as their naval representative in Great Britain an able, shrewd, and resourceful man in James D. Bulloch. Bulloch's was a stupendously difficult task, requiring the exercise of intelligence, diplomacy, intrigue, tact, and business ability, all of which talents he possessed in abundance. Great Britain, though at times apparently friendly, never accorded formal recognition to the government of the Confederate States of America; and its foreign office sternly insisted on a strict observance of the letter of the laws guaranteeing British neutrality.

The United States minister to the court of Saint James during these turbulent times was the astute Charles Francis Adams, whose sagacity and zeal and never-tiring watchfulness placed every possible stumbling-block in the way of Confederate activities. Not only was he politely but relentlessly insistent on Great Britain's strict enforcement of Queen Victoria's proclamation of neutrality, but whenever the Crown seemed inclined to laxity in this direction, Adams did not hesitate to insist on official attention to instances of apparent infractions of the laws which had been uncovered by his own agents. Every movement of Bulloch was shadowed. His known agents and associates were watched wherever they went. Very little was done by the Confederate agents in Great Britain that did not sooner or later come to the attention of the Argus-eyed Adams.

Despite this network of surveillance, the Confederate naval representative was able by adroit maneuvering to conclude a number of negotiations with British ship builders, but sad experience had taught him that in playing this dangerous game with his crafty adversaries no amount of caution was too much.

Notable among Bulloch's accomplishments had been the building and outfitting of the Alabama, the Confederate raiding cruiser which under the command of Admiral Semmes scourged the shipping of the United States and almost swept the Stars and Stripes off the seven seas. The Northern press cried "Piracy!" but the Confederate policy of destroying commerce carriers was based soundly on the principles enunciated by President Madison during the War of 1812, and the men engaged in it were regularly commissioned officers of a government which had been recognized as a belligerent. The charge of piracy could not be sustained, and the Alabama roved the seas sinking one Yankee merchant vessel after another and occasionally having a successful brush with a Yankee warship.

For two years the Alabama continued its career of destruction, but in June, 1864, she put into neutral Cherbourg for repairs and refitting. Semmes, who had a penchant for flowery phrases, likened her to "the weary foxhound, limping back after a long chase, footsore and longing for quiet and repose." But there was to be no quiet and repose for the Alabama. Within a few days after her arrival in Cherbourg the United States cruiser Kearsarge, commanded by <u>Captain Winslow</u>, took up a position off the breakwater outside the harbor, obviously daring the Confederate vessel to come out. Prompted by a medieval sense of chivalry, Semmes made the fatal error of accepting the challenge. He formally and courteously notified Captain Winslow that he would come out and fight him as soon as he had finished coaling.

So on the morning of June 19, 1864, the Alabama stood out to sea, and both vessels steamed away to a point seven miles off shore where, before a crowd of spectators gathered on the French coast, they staged the naval duel which has become famous in maritime history. For more than two hours, as the two cruisers steamed at full speed in a circular course and the cliffs of the Channel re-echoed with the booming of the guns, they poured point-blank broadsides into each other.

There was good gunnery on both sides that day, but the big eleven-inch shells from the well-aimed guns of the Kearsarge finally proved too much for her adversary. A Confederate gunner, sponging his piece, happened to glance over the side of the Alabama, and the sight he saw chilled him with terror. There in the Alabama's planking, right at the waterline, gaped a jagged opening. With every roll of the sea, water gushed into her hold, and despite frantic

10

efforts to repair the breach, the Confederate cruiser sank.

Throughout the Northern states there was a great wave of fervent exultation at the destruction of the Alabama. Yankee shipowners breathed their relief. Correspondingly, the Confederate authorities recognized immediately that the destroyed cruiser must be replaced promptly. In England, Bulloch knew without being told that the task of replacement must fall on him.

CHAPTER TWO

HATCHING A HAWK

————————————

THE ALABAMA had done her work with a wonderfully thorough and devastating efficiency. No less than fifty-four merchant vessels flying the United States flag had been destroyed with their cargoes. Marine insurance rates on ships of American registry had skyrocketed to prohibitive levels, and most of the surviving merchantmen were discreetly riding in their home harbors or in neutral ports. The Alabama had almost swept the American flag off the ocean.

The Confederate authorities realized, however, that the news of the sinking of the famous raider would take some of that paralyzing chill out of the hearts of the Yankee shipowners; it was imperative, they felt, to send another raiding Confederate cruiser to maintain the terror created by the Alabama.

In London Bulloch knew without waiting to hear from Richmond that the emergency called for prompt action. Bulloch was able to move swiftly, for he had made it his business to maintain in his mind a fairly complete memorandum of all the ships afloat that were capable of being adapted to the needs of the Confederacy. He could almost call the roll of the merchant vessels that moved in and out of British ports. Facing the task of replacing the destroyed Alabama, he ran over the list. Of all the ships there was one that stood out plainly as the ideal vessel, the sleekest, trimmest craft he had ever seen, the one ship he would most desire to have under the Confederate flag.

Bulloch had stumbled upon the Sea King during the autumn of 1863, when he was in Glasgow accompanied by Lieutenant Robert R. Carter looking for a small steamer to be used for blockade-running. While tramping along the docks, taking a surreptitious but none the less thorough inventory of the vessels then in the Clyde, they suddenly came upon her, and both involuntarily gasped in admiration.

She had just been completed in the yards of Stevens & Sons, and her new paint glistened in the sunlight. She was a full-rigged sailing ship with rolling top-sails, but she was of the new composite type, being equipped with auxiliary steam engines and with a lifting screw which could be taken up out of the water when the engines were not in use. Barely able to suppress their eager enthusiasm, they inquired about her specifications and equipment. She measured, they found, 227 feet from bowsprit to stern and 35 feet in the beam, and was of 1,160 tons builder's measurement. Her frames and beams were iron, but she was planked from keel to gunwale with six inches of East India teak. She had ample accommodations for officers of all grades. Her between-decks afforded seven and a half feet of head room, and she had large air-ports, having been fitted under

13

government inspection for the transport of British troops to the colonies. Her engines were of the latest and best type, direct acting, with two cylinders forty-seven inches in diameter having two feet nine inches of stroke and a nominal horsepower of 220, but an indicated development of 850.

"What a cruiser she would make!" exclaimed Bulloch covetously as soon as his eye fell upon her, and Carter promptly and heartily agreed that here was a vessel ideally adapted to conversion into a warship. They looked admiringly at her trim lines and her unmistakable indications of power and speed. But all the air castles they started building were promptly toppled down when, upon investigation, they learned that she was the property of the London, Bombay & Calcutta Steamship Company and was then being loaded for her maiden voyage to New Zealand and China, a trip which would keep her at sea for ten or twelve months. To their sorrow they were forced to realize that she was out of reach of the Confederates, temporarily at least; but she made an indelible impression on Bulloch's mind, and he filed away neatly in one of the crowded pigeonholes of his methodical brain the essential facts about her.

So it was that nearly a year later, when he was confronted with the necessity for replacing the Alabama, his memory promptly brought back the picture of that trim East India merchantman swinging at her hawsers in the Clyde. Bulloch was a practical man. He knew that it was vain to hope that it would be possible on short notice to find and purchase that vessel, for it would be like looking for a nautical needle in a maritime haystack. He could, however, use the Sea King as an ideal, and so when he called into consultation a friendly London shipping broker and started him on a trip to scour the Clyde and the principal ports of Scotland and England looking for an available vessel, he gave a detailed description of the Sea King as an example of the ideal craft for the purpose in view.

The agent entrusted with this confidential scouting trip was Richard Wright, a native of England and thus not subject to the suspicion of nosey British officers. It happened, however, that he was also the father-in-law of Charles K. Prioleau, of Charleston, South Carolina, who was then the managing partner in Liverpool of the banking firm of Fraser, Trenholm & Company, which handled all of the Confederacy's financial transactions in Great Britain. Wright's sympathies, not unnaturally, were secretly with the Confederates, and he entered wholeheartedly into the task assigned him. From one port to another he went, inspecting the available craft, but nothing he could find exactly suited the requirements. Then, one day, plodding disconsolately along the Glasgow waterfront, almost ready to give up the quest, he saw looming up in front of him the graceful prow of the Sea King herself, just back from China and New Zealand. The waterfront was buzzing with excited comment over the speed record she had established.

"A sea king she is for a fact," remarked one of her crew to Wright as he stood admiring her. "She made 330 miles in twenty-four hours on her homeward trip. Her log shows it."

And so she had. She was a greyhound of the seas for those days, and the shipmasters of the Clyde, not given to extravagant praise, were loud in their plaudits.

When Wright found her at her berth, her cargo of tea had just been discharged, and a thorough inspection was easy. Immediately he sent Bulloch a code telegram informing him of his rare good fortune and advising him to purchase her before she was put under engagement for another voyage. Bulloch lost no time in authorizing the deal, and on September 20 there was registered the transfer of the Sea King to Richard Wright for £45,000 sterling. Lloyd's inspectors went over her and pronounced her "a capital ship in every respect," and she was moved to London and unostentatiously docked there.

Meanwhile Secretary Mallory's office in Richmond was boiling with excitement over the matter of a successor to the Alabama. It was assumed by all as a matter of course that such a successor would be commissioned as soon as possible, and it was taken for granted that Bulloch would already be making his preparations accordingly. But there was considerable discussion among navy officials about what a new cruiser would do once she was put into commission.

"I am afraid," observed Mallory with a wry smile, "that Admiral Semmes has left us very little material for destruction. A new broom is not very useful in a well swept room."

But stationed in Secretary Mallory's office at the time was a young man of vision and imagination, Lieutenant Robert R. Carter—one of the Virginia

16

Carters, from Shirley on the James. He was the same
Lieutenant Carter who had been on Bulloch's staff
and was with him when the Sea King was first discovered in Glasgow. Since then he had been active in
running the blockade at Wilmington, and more
recently had been on the Secretary's staff in Richmond. Mulling over what Mallory had said about the
lack of a definite program of action for the new
cruiser, he had what he considered a brilliant inspira-
tion, and he took it to his superior's office.

"You will recall," he said to the Secretary, "that
after I graduated from the Academy, I served on the
scientific expedition sent to the North Pacific in 1855.
We visited all those localities frequented by the New
England whaling fleet and followed some of their
routes. I know where the whalers go, how they get
there, and how long they stay. Here's my idea: Why
not send our new cruiser directly to the whaling
grounds—the Sea of Okhotsk, the Bering, and the
Arctic—hunt down the Yankee whalers and wipe
them out? It would be the greatest blow we could possibly strike at the Yankees' pocketbook, and that's
where they are most sensitive."

Mallory was interested by the novel suggestion,
but cautiously refrained from giving his immediate
endorsement to the idea. So the enthusiastic Carter
brought up reinforcements. Located in Richmond in
charge of the Naval Ordnance Bureau was Lieutenant John M. Brooke. He too had been an officer in
the old navy, and had been a shipmate of Carter's
on that scientific voyage to the Pacific. He immediately envisioned the possibilities of the proposed

17

arctic raid and joined Carter in importuning Mallory to let loose this thunderbolt of destruction in a quarter where it was least expected.

"They think they are safe, away up there in the ice," Brooke argued. "But why shouldn't we go up there after them? The right kind of a vessel could make its way through those floes, I believe. It would be risky business, but it could be done. And just think of the howls in New Bedford and Boston and New York—and in Washington—when they learn that their whaling fleet has been wiped out by a Rebel raider. There is no one thing we could do today that would strike more fear into Northern hearts."

Before the irresistible enthusiasm of his youthful aides Mallory's objections melted away, and soon he grew as eager as they in contemplation of the proposed raid. His mind readily grasped the magnitude and far-reaching potentialities of the audacious scheme, and without delay he rushed Lieutenant Carter to England to convey to Bulloch the Confederate government's formal instructions to organize the proposed expedition against the whalers.

Carter's conception of the scheme had extended to a consideration of the kind of vessel needed for the purpose; and it is significant of the outward impressiveness of the Sea King that his mind unerringly harked back to that sleek composite ship which he and Bulloch had seen in the Clyde a year before. So attractive a picture did he paint of the ship in talking to Mallory that the Secretary's official instructions were accompanied by the suggestion that Bulloch purchase that particular vessel for the purpose if possible, and when Carter arrived in Liverpool on September 28 with his specific orders for the arctic raid, he was thrilled to find that the Sea King was already safely in possession of the staid and reliable British friend who provided a mask of innocence for the Confederates' extra-legal activities.

Bulloch, appreciating the value of Carter's first-hand information regarding the whaling field, set him to work preparing a memorandum of cruising directions for the commander of the expedition. Carter soon produced a detailed paper on the periodical movements of the whaling fleet and added a set of the Whale Charts published by Commander Matthew Fontaine Maury in connection with his *Physical Geography of the Sea.*

In the meanwhile Bulloch proceeded with the work of arranging to get the Sea King ready for her conversion, a work which was hampered to a great degree by the very excellence of the ship itself. She was the only vessel of her type in Great Britain and therefore a constant object of attention and interest in the London docks to which she had been moved. It was so obvious to Bulloch that the Sea King was ideally adapted to conversion into a war vessel that he was sure she must soon attract the attention of Adams's spies.

An awkward obstacle was the fact that he himself could not afford to be seen on the vessel or even in her vicinity, as that would immediately direct suspicion against her. No one who had ever had the slightest known connection with the Confederates in England could be permitted to go near her, but yet she must be made ready for her voyage with as little delay as possible. The Sea King at her berth in the Thames was a beautiful vessel and a valuable piece of marine property, but she was of no use to the Confederate States of America, her undercover owners, until she could be placed in commission as a duly-authorized Confederate war vessel and put to work on the high seas.

The neutrality laws expressly and effectively prevented the transfer of the ship to the Confederate government in a British port. The laws also forbade the outfitting or equipping of the vessel for purposes of war. The foreign enlistment act made it impossible to recruit a crew on British soil. These were the major obstacles which Bulloch must hurdle before the peaceful Sea King could be transformed into an armed cruiser flying the Confederate flag. But Bulloch had grown accustomed to obstacles, and by swift and adroit work he had the cruiser in commission and under the Stars and Bars on the open seas within thirty days.

CHAPTER THREE

RENDEZVOUS ON THE
HIGH SEAS

B ULLOCH'S SOLUTION of the perplexities confront-
ing him was simple enough in design, but promised to be difficult of execution. The Sea King
could not be transferred, outfitted, and manned as a
cruiser in a neutral port, and all the ports of the Confederate States were effectively closed. It seemed obvious, therefore, that the only feasible program was
to have all these transactions take place on the high
seas.

So Bulloch's plan was carefully laid: The Sea
King would clear from London on an apparently
legitimate commercial voyage, carefully doing nothing to excite suspicion. Once at sea she would proceed, not to the destination named in her clearance
papers, but to the Madeira Islands off the coast of
Morocco. There she would be met by a supply vessel
carrying the necessary armament, supplies, and officers. There, on the open sea, the vessel could be
legally sold by her dummy owner to the government
of the Confederate States of America. And there the

British merchantman Sea King would be formally and officially re-born into a Confederate cruiser for which Bulloch had already selected a name—the Shenandoah.

So far as the Sea King herself was concerned, Bulloch was keenly aware that, whatever her ultimate character might be, it was essential that she maintain a lily-white appearance of innocence so long as she was in a British port. So Wright, in whom the title was still vested, had her ballasted with coal, took on provisions for a twelve-months cruise, and formally cleared her for Bombay.

The Sea King had been placed under the command of Captain Peter S. Corbett. Corbett was a native Englishman, but he had commanded a blockade-runner earlier in the war, and the Confederates had reason to be confident of his friendliness. He established himself at the Sailors' Home lodging house on the Thames waterfront and passed the news about the neighborhood of the East India docks that he was enlisting a crew "for a voyage to Bombay or any port of the Indian Ocean, China Sea or Japan, for a term of not to exceed two years." There was nothing on the surface to indicate that the Sea King was preparing for anything but a law-abiding cruise, and there was a steady trickle of seafaring men to the Sailors' Home to talk with Captain Corbett.

"Are you married or single?" was one of the first questions Corbett asked every applicant, making no secret of the fact that he preferred single men. But it was to be a long voyage, so that excited no suspicion, and the crew list rapidly filled up. The ship had two 18-pound swivel guns mounted on her decks, but that was customary equipment for an East India-man in those days, and their presence aroused no comment.

While the work of preparing the Sea King for her mythical voyage to Bombay and the Orient was pro-gressing in orderly fashion, Bulloch was engaged in a quiet hunt for a smaller vessel to be used as the tender, which could be loaded secretly with guns and ammunition and supplies and, with the officers of the cruise-to-be as passengers, sail from some other port and meet the Sea King at the appointed rendezvous off the Madeiras. With characteristic thriftiness, Bulloch desired to obtain for this purpose a vessel which, after it had played its part in the Sea King's drama, could then earn its expenses or perhaps even recoup the cost of purchase by running the block-ade, and he instructed his broker to make a search for such a vessel.

Within a few days the broker notified Bulloch that he had discovered in Liverpool what seemed to be just what was needed, a new iron screw-steamer, fore-and-aft rigged for sailing, named the Laurel, which had been built for the packet service between Liverpool and the Irish coast. Bulloch boldly took a trip on the Laurel as a passenger from Liverpool to Queenstown and return, during the course of which he found op-portunity to examine her closely for the purpose of acquiring a first-hand estimate of her suitability. The trip was reassuring. The Laurel was a strong, sea-worthy vessel of moderate draft, steaming at thirteen knots, and apparently well adapted to running the blockade after serving as the Sea King's tender. Accordingly she was purchased, in the name of Henry Lafore, a British citizen. He put her in the hands of a shipping agent in Liverpool, who proceeded to advertise her for a voyage to Matamoras, via Nassau and Havana, to take freight and a limited number of passengers.

Mr. Lafore, however, took the precaution of informing the shipping agent in advance what amount of freight and how many passengers would be forthcoming. Everything was strictly legal. The agent would not for anything connive at violating the British neutrality regulations. But any unsuspecting person who innocently applied for passage to Matamoras or Nassau or Havana or who wished to ship any freight to those ports was regretfully informed that the passenger list was already filled and the cargo space all booked.

Speedily the work of loading the Laurel's freight proceeded. There were a remarkable number of heavy crates—crates which were conspicuously labeled "Machinery," but which contained guns and gun carriages. There were eight guns, six large eight-inch 68-pounders and two small Whitworth 32-pounders, cast by Randolph & Elders of Glasgow the year before for the privateer Pampero which had been built for the Confederates but seized by the British authorities before she was finished and outfitted. Then there were barrels of powder marked "Glassware—Handle With Care," heavy boxes of carbines and pistols and cutlasses, shot and shell, boxes of clothing

—gray uniforms with bright brass buttons—food-stuffs, and other supplies.

Gravely the shipping agents issued bills of lading for the machinery and glassware as it was loaded, and also took from Bulloch's agent the passage money for the "passengers," writing out all the tickets under various assumed names. To the clerks in the office, and to any inquisitive person who might come nosing around, there was every outward indication that everything in connection with the sailing of the Laurel was proceeding in the routine course of legitimate business. Beneath the surface, however, there was fiddlestring tension as the loading of the vessel proceeded, and the passengers—the officers and the selected nucleus of a crew for the new cruiser—kept out of sight in widely separated lodging houses in Liverpool and twiddled their thumbs as they waited for sailing orders.

By no means the least of the problems connected with the outfitting of the new cruiser had been the selection of the staff of officers which was now assembling clandestinely in Liverpool. In the first place it was necessary to have a competent commander, a man of experience, capacity, poise, and self-reliance. The Shenandoah would be out on its own responsibility for many months, perhaps years, and she must be in charge of a man who was not only a skilled mariner but a resourceful and capable executive as well. Furthermore, it should be some one who was not known in England, so that he might be brought to Liverpool and remain there without attracting attention until all plans were completed.

Secretary Mallory selected for this all-important post Lieutenant James I. Waddell, a native of North Carolina, forty years old, who had behind him twenty-three years of efficient service in the United States Navy. In 1858 his ability had been recognized by an appointment as assistant professor of navigation in the Naval Academy at Annapolis, a position which he filled commendably until restored to active service in 1860. When the war broke out in the spring of 1861, he was serving with the East India squadron, but as soon as he heard of the secession of North Carolina he mailed in his resignation from St. Helena. His resignation was never officially accepted, however, and beside his name on the records of the United States Navy there stands today the single word "Dismissed."

Having sent in his resignation, Waddell felt in honor bound to leave the ship on which he considered himself no longer an officer, but having done so, he experienced great difficulty in getting back home. At length, however, he succeeded in running the blockade into Wilmington in February, 1862, and upon his arrival in Richmond he was promptly rewarded with a lieutenant's commission in the fledgling Confederate Navy and put in charge of the defenses of Richmond at Drewry's Bluff on the James River. Later he was transferred to Charleston and put in command of the harbor there, and here, in 1864, he received his orders to report to Commodore Barron, in charge of the Confederate naval forces in Europe. Running the blockade, he proceeded to Paris, where

Barron issued him a commission as Lieutenant-commander, told him briefly of the plans to commission a new cruiser to replace the Alabama, and ordered him to report to Bulloch in Liverpool for further specific instructions.

Meanwhile the men who were to constitute the official family of the Shenandoah were being secretly assembled in Liverpool, most of them unaware of the presence of the others. All were men who had never before been in England—faces unfamiliar to Yankee spies there. Three veterans of the Alabama were brought over from Cherbourg. The other young officers ran the blockade out of Southern ports to France. All had been ordered by Commodore Barron to report to Bulloch in Liverpool, but none was aware of the nature of his future assignment. They had all had naval training or experience of some kind, and several of them had attended the Academy at Annapolis, but on the whole they were pitifully immature and inexperienced in view of the desperate adventure contemplated, and two of them had never before been to sea.

Lieutenant Whittle, who was to be second in command, was young, but he was an experienced and reliable officer, a man of proved discretion and ability. He came of seafaring stock, his father being then a captain in the Confederate naval service and a veteran officer of the old navy. He was himself a graduate of the Naval Academy in the class of 1858, but he had resigned his commission in 1861 to cast his lot with the Confederacy. He had been one of the officers of the gunboat Nashville when she ran the blockade in 1861 to carry the famous Mason and Slidell to Bermuda, and he was on this little vessel when she proceeded to Liverpool—the first craft to show the Confederate flag in British waters. Later young Whittle was in command of the Nashville, his most brilliant exploit having been the occasion when he took her out through the blockade at Morehead City and back through the blockading cordon into Charleston harbor. To him was assigned the duty of shipping on board the Sea King as her supercargo just before she sailed from London. It was extremely dangerous to have anybody connected with the Confederacy seen in the neighborhood of the ship while she was in London, but it was essential that some competent Southern officer sail aboard her and utilize the time between London and Funchal in familiarizing himself with the ship and devising plans for her transformation into a vessel of war.

In command of the Laurel on her outward voyage was another young man in his twenties, Lieutenant J. F. Ramsey. He held a commission in the Confederate Navy, but he had also served for several years in the British merchant service and held a Board of Trade certificate of competency as master, and was therefore eligible to command what purported to be a British merchant ship. A contemporary described him as "very smart and wide awake," and a smart and wide-awake man was needed to carry out the Laurel's part in the program.

Captain Waddell was in personal charge of the Laurel's passengers, soon to be his officers on the

Shenandoah, and his was the immediate duty of keeping in touch with them in Liverpool and seeing that they boarded the tender at the proper time. A close-mouthed man of undistinguished appearance, he attracted no undue attention as he lived quietly with his wife in the rooms on Clegg Street they had taken upon their arrival in Liverpool. The young officers were scattered in lodgings throughout the city and instructed to live quietly and avoid contact with Confederate agents. Above all, they were to stay away from the Adelphi Hotel, which was "crowded with Yankee spies."

There had also been brought to Liverpool a few picked men from the crew of the late Alabama who were designed to constitute a nucleus for the new working force when organized at the place of rendezvous. It was no secret that it was hoped to recruit a crew for the Shenandoah from the men of the Sea King and the Laurel, once the former was officially transferred to the service of the Confederate States, and George Harwood, a native of England, who had served as chief boatswain's mate on the Alabama, was sent along to serve as boatswain and use his influence with a crew which must necessarily be composed mostly of Englishmen. There were also Andrew Bachman, boatswain's mate; Henry Alcott, sailmaker; John O'Shea, carpenter; John Guy and William Crawford, gunner's mates; and William Simpson, cockswain of the captain's gig. Even with a makeshift crew, the Confederates would be certain of dependable men in the key positions.

At last all the preliminary arrangements were completed, both in London and in Liverpool, and the vessels were ready to sail.

On October 6 the letter of instruction was sent to Lieutenant Whittle ordering him to proceed to London that night and be at Wood's Hotel the following morning. There he was to receive oral instructions from the Confederacy's undercover man who had been detailed to take him on board the Sea King without attracting attention and introduce him to Captain Corbett.

Wright had already given Corbett a bill of sale for the vessel, authorizing him to sell her at any time within six months for the sum of £45,000, and just before sailing the captain was notified that he was to shape his course for the Bay of Funchal, Madeira, and meet the Laurel there on October 17. Corbett was specifically told that it was important that the Sea King should not be reported after leaving London, and that he was not to exchange signals with passing ships, as there was no use in exciting speculation why a vessel bound for Bombay was so far off her normal course.

Whittle boarded the Sea King in the dead of night on the seventh, and early the next morning she hauled up her anchor and dropped down the Thames—out past two Yankee warships ominously steaming up and down at the river's mouth, on into the Channel, and away on the first leg of her long and turbulent cruise.

As soon as the Sea King had departed, a code telegram was flashed to Lieutenant Ramsey in Liverpool instructing him to get everything ready and set out at once for Funchal. Immediately after dark that night Ramsey sent out a messenger who hurried from hotel to boardinghouse to apartment, notifying the passengers that the time had come for them to get aboard the Laurel. Accordingly they made their way, singly and without any appearance of concerted action or knowledge of each other's movements, to Prince's Landing Stage, where a steam tug was waiting to convey them on board the steamer. Their trunks, packed with their uniforms, side arms, and other effects had already gone aboard the Laurel, nailed up in wooden boxes to disguise them as freight.

It was a chilly October evening, with a heavy mist drenching the city, as the Laurel's passengers plodded down the wet, slippery streets to the landing stage, each feigning to have no knowledge of the others who were proceeding to the same destination. Even on board the launch they kept up the profession of being entire strangers to each other, silently accepting the bogus receipts issued in assumed names which stated that they had each paid the sum of £32 for cabin passage to the port of Havana. Before midnight the entire complement of passengers had been checked in on the Laurel and conducted to their staterooms, and early in the morning she got up steam and slid silently down the Mersey.

The Yankee spies had not been idle all this time. They had an uncanny genius for scenting Confederate activities, and somehow or other at the last minute they got wind of the sinister nature of the contents of the Laurel's crates of machinery and barrels of glassware. On October 7 the American consul in Liverpool, Thomas H. Dudley, wrote to Adams in London that his agents had been watching the Laurel and that he had come to suspect that she was destined to become a Confederate privateer. "Her movements are most suspicious," he wrote. "She has taken on a number of cases containing guns, etc., and she has shipped 21 more seamen than are required for a vessel of her class. I have heard that a former lieutenant of the privateer Georgia is to go out on her; and I also understand that the notorious Semmes himself is in London and will command her when she sails."

This was hitting pretty close to the mark, but the warning came too late for any preventive steps to be taken, and the Laurel went on her way undisturbed.

It developed later that the United States agents in London had also begun to smell a rat before the Sea King sailed. In some way they had discovered that a Confederate vessel was being clandestinely outfitted there but despite their most frantic efforts they could not find out her name. The ownership of every vessel in the docks was carefully checked, and in the course of this investigation the secretary of the legation in London wrote to Mr. Dudley asking him if he knew anything about Richard Wright in whose name was registered a likely looking merchantman called the Sea King. Dudley supplied all the damning facts about Wright's relationship to Prioleau, the Confederate banker, but by that time the Sea King had sailed.

There were only two American warships in English waters at this time, and when the alarm was first sounded, they had been stationed off the mouth of the Thames on police duty. In the absence of any definite information, the cruisers had been ordered to scrutinize every vessel that came out into the Channel and stop and examine any that looked suspicious. The Sea King must have been under a lucky star, or else she had a protecting appearance of innocence. At any rate, she sailed by the watch-dogs undisturbed. But the next morning the sentinel warship stopped and interrogated an innocent Spanish merchantman. Her master, after great difficulty, succeeded in convincing the Yankees that he was not a Rebel cruiser in disguise, but while they wrangled the Sea King was rolling down toward the Madeiras.

After the Laurel and the Sea King were both safely at sea the Southern sympathizers in England made no further effort at concealment, but boldly boasted that the world would soon be hearing of the exploits of a new Confederate raider. Adams promptly ordered his two warships off in pursuit of the vessels under suspicion, and then wrote to Secretary Seward in Washington to convey to him the unpleasant news that a new Confederate cruiser was probably at large. Adams had himself sized up the Sea King when she was first launched and put into the merchant service, for he said in his letter, "She is the same vessel that I saw at Glasgow on the occasion of one of my visits to that town last year. I regarded her then as a most likely steamer for the purposes of a privateer and so reported to you at the time." He closed with the prophetic remark: "If I mistake not, she will prove herself a dangerous and destructive craft to our commerce."

Bulloch's work in connection with this particular expedition was now done, and well done. He had successfully outwitted Adams and his spies, and he permitted a note of pride to creep into the opening lines of his report to Secretary Mallory: "I have the great satisfaction of reporting the safe departure on the 8th instant of the ship described in my dispatch of September 16th; and now the entire expedition is far away at sea, beyond the reach of interference on the part of any United States authority in Europe."

With his report to the Secretary in Richmond, Bulloch was able to close his file on the Sea King. But on the high seas Captain Waddell's troubles were just beginning. His was now the duty of bringing the Laurel and the Sea King together and placing the new cruiser in commission. Ahead of him lay long months of desperate adventure, in strange seas, with an inexperienced and unfamiliar staff of officers, and with a crew whose numbers and efficiency were yet unknown.

Waddell, in his bunk on the Laurel, lay awake late that night.

CHAPTER FOUR

THE BIRTH OF A CRUISER

As THE LAUREL wallowed down the Irish Sea and out into the open Atlantic, Captain Waddell sat in the cabin immersed in deep and apprehensive introspection. Impressed with the immensity of his appointed task, his brow wrinkled as he pored over the charts of the Pacific, the Okhotsk, and the Arctic. He pulled nervously at the ends of his graying moustache as he reread his letters of instruction and pondered over the unpredictable difficulties lying ahead of him.

Commander Barron's orders, sent to him from Paris, had been terse but clear: "When the vessel under your command is ready for sea you will sail on a cruise in the region of ocean already indicated to you in our personal interview. The charts which have been sent you are the best sailing directions which you can have. Your position is an important one, not only with reference to the immediate results to the enemy's property, but from the fact that neutral rights may frequently arise under it. Reliance, however, is placed in your judgment and discretion for meeting and promptly disposing of such questions.

You will not hesitate to assume responsibility when the interests of your country may demand it, and should your judgment ever hesitate in seeking the solution of any difficulty it may be aided by the reflection that you are to do the enemy's property the greatest injury in the shortest time."

Bulloch also had provided him with a letter of instructions. "You are," he wrote, "about to proceed upon a cruise in the far-distant Pacific, into the seas and among the islands frequented by the great American whaling fleet, a source of abundant wealth to our enemies and a nursery for their seamen. It is hoped that you may be able to greatly damage and disperse that fleet, even if you do not succeed in utterly destroying it. Considering the extent of ocean to be sailed over, the necessarily incomplete equipment of your ship at the beginning of the cruise, and your approaching isolation from the aid and comfort of your countrymen, a letter of specific instructions would be wholly superfluous."

Whereupon Bulloch, having eloquently disclaimed the need for giving instructions, proceeded to do so in several thousand words of definite directions as to what the commander should do and what he should not do, like an anxious father starting a small boy out on his first trip to school. Fortunately for Waddell, however, his sailing orders were epitomized in a laconic memorandum sent out from Richmond which presented the whole scheme in a detached and impersonal manner:

"A fast vessel with auxiliary steam power, leaving the meridian of the Cape of Good Hope on the 1st of

January, would reach Sydney in Australia in forty days, adding twenty days for incidental interruptions; and, leaving the coast of Australia on the 1st of March, passing through the whaling ground and between New Zealand and New Holland and the Caroline group, touching at Ascension, and allowing thirty days for incidental interruptions, would reach the Ladrone Islands by the 1st of June. She would then, visiting the Bonin Islands, Sea of Japan, Okhotsk and North Pacific, be in a position about the 15th of September, north of the Island of Oahu, distant from 60 to 100 miles, to intercept the North Pacific whaling fleet bound to Oahu with the products of the summer cruise."

There was the whole campaign in a nutshell, and the commander pricked off the named landmarks on his chart and carefully computed the probable sailing time. Dreamily he gazed out over the blue water as he read over the names of these far-off and unfamiliar places—places where the Stars and Bars would come as a strange, new flag and where the war between the North and South was but a dim and shadowy thing.

But Captain Waddell had little time for dreaming. Aside from studying his instructions and roughly formulating his plans, there were various little technical details to which his attention must immediately be given. Now at last free from the troublesome interference of the neutrality laws, he could give to each of the officers the official, written notification to report to him for duty, a formality which could not be performed on British soil. This done, the trunks were opened, and the new Confederate uniforms, made in

Paris, were parceled out to the men, so that the new cruiser could be taken over in formal style when the time came. And George Harwood had to be given his appointment as boatswain and instructed as to the service he was expected to perform in inducing enlistments from the crews of the Sea King and Laurel. There was plenty to keep Waddell occupied.

Meanwhile the young officers, now that they need no longer play at the game of concealing their identities, were getting acquainted with each other and improving the opportunity for jollification. Those who had served on board the Alabama spun, for the edification of their inexperienced mates, endless and highly colored yarns of the alluring possibilities of life on a roving Confederate man-of-war. Perhaps some of these youthful veterans thought sometimes of the heartbreaking ending of the Alabama's cruise. They could not well forget that tragic day off Cherbourg when the shot-riddled cruiser dived to the bottom and left them struggling for life in the choppy sea. But this was no time to be thinking of death or speculating on the possible hazards of the cruise on which they were embarking. Battle and murder and death might lie ahead of them, but now they were alive and young and thrilled with the immediate adventure of living. So they swapped their yarns and drank their grog and lightly passed away their time while Commander Waddell in the cabin pored over his charts and chewed the end of his pencil.

On the morning of October 16, six days out from Liverpool, the island of Madeira rose mistily on the horizon, and before noon of that day they dropped anchor in the Bay of Funchal, a little ahead of the pre-arranged schedule. The first order given upon arrival in the bay was that there was to be positively no communication with the shore except that which was officially required between the commander and the customs officials, and the refilling of the coal bunkers. There was no shore leave permitted for either officers or men, and they were forced to lounge restlessly on deck and wistfully view the attractions of the close but inaccessible island, the tall towers of the church of Nostra Senhora del Monte on the summit of its towering cliff, the miniature Gibraltar-like fortress hewn out of the living stone, the clean, shining public buildings, and the glistening green foliage of the trees. But, after all, this was no sightseeing cruise. They were there for only one purpose, to board the vessel on which they were to carry the Confederate ensign around the world on a voyage of destruction, and there was not a man on board who did not long for a sight of the Sea King more keenly than he did for any of the attractions of Madeira.

One of Captain Waddell's first steps after dropping anchor was to station a lookout to report the appearance of all vessels coming in sight off the harbor. This watch was kept up day and night, orders being given that if any passing vessel hoisted flags or showed signal lights, the commander should be promptly notified of the character of the vessel and the signals.

Meanwhile the Laurel was coaled and made ready for sea, her papers perforce being left at the customs house until the time of departure. Captain Waddell went ashore and cashed a draft for £5,000 to serve as his sailing fund, and everything was ready for immediate action as soon as the Sea King should put in her appearance. The authorities ashore had been told that the passenger list was made up of a lot of emigrants from Poland bound for the West Indies, and that they did not care to come ashore for a visit but preferred to remain on the ship.

After two days had passed, some apprehension began to be felt at the Sea King's failure to arrive, and vague fears arose that something might have interfered with her departure from London. The United States consul (United States consuls were an inordinately suspicious and meddlesome lot in those days) thought it peculiar that the Laurel should continue to lie at anchor so long for no apparent reason after her coaling was finished, and as a precaution he asked the Portuguese authorities to detain her for examination. He was not able, however, to offer any justifiable reason for such detention, aside from his unsupported suspicion that something was wrong, so the Portuguese port officials declined to take the risk of offending the British government whose flag the Laurel flew. Waddell and his companions, however, were in an agony of uneasy suspense, knowing that they were suspects themselves and imagining all sorts of dire fates which might have befallen the Sea King.

But at last, during the first watch of October 18— a clear, calm, and moonlit night—a ship-rigged vessel came into sight outside the harbor and within a short distance of the Funchal anchorage, steaming slowly and showing her signal lights. The display of such lights was not an uncommon courtesy for passing vessels or those returning from a voyage to extend to those in harbor, the object being to announce the vessel's name and the tidings of her safety, to be communicated to those interested in the progress of her voyage. But this mysterious ship gave no sign of her identity, nor did she enter the harbor. Instead she steamed slowly on and soon passed out of sight south of the port, leaving a buzz of excited comment on the deck of the Laurel. Was it the Sea King? None of them had ever seen her, and they could only guess.

"She is three-master, square-rigged," reported the man with the glass. "She has a round stern and a poop."

"That sounds like her description," said Waddell. "It must be her. But where has she gone?"

Within a short while his question was answered. The stranger ship came into sight off the port, steaming back in the direction from which she had come. She still burned her signal lights, but still gave no sign of her identity, and as she silently disappeared north of the port, subdued murmurs of "That's her!" broke out among the eager men gathered anxiously along the Laurel's rail.

That was a night of tingling suspense on board the supply ship, one of enforced waiting for morning to come. It was contrary to the rules of the port to leave the harbor between sunset and dawn, for the formality of departure could not be executed until the steamer's papers were returned by the customs officer. So there was nothing to do but wait for morning. There was but fitful sleeping on the Laurel that night as she rolled impatiently at anchor.

Early the next morning a messenger was hurried ashore to the customs officer requesting him to bring the ship's papers aboard so that she might cast off. While the customs boat was on its way from the quay to the Laurel, the black steamer came into sight again from the north, now boldly flying from her masthead signal flags giving the Laurel's official number. These were joyfully recognized and answered by a display of the same number signal, and the pseudo-passengers on board the Laurel pulled off their wide-brimmed straw hats and threw them into the air as they cheered the sight of the arriving vessel. Even the natives in the bumboats jostling about the sides of the little steamer realized that something extraordinary was happening, that there was something peculiar and sinister in the behavior of the mysterious black vessel which would not come into the anchorage. Prompted by a strange premonition, they cried, "Otro Alabama!" (Another Alabama!)

Fires had been kindled in the Laurel's furnaces at daybreak, chain had been hove in to a short stay, and she swung restlessly to a single anchor. The instant the customs officer had finished his perfunctory business and climbed down the side, her anchor was tripped and, with the Yankee consul fuming on the quay, she stood to sea in pursuit of the black vessel. Rolling heavily through the thick weather, she began swiftly to overhaul the long, slim steamer, whose engines had been accommodatingly slowed, and as Commander Waddell watched her eagerly through his glass, he soon descried on her stern the welcome words: "Sea King—London."

As he read that inscription, a strange fancy flashed across the commander's oppressed mind: Was it an omen? Was his new command to be indeed a king of the sea? Captain Waddell was a pious man, and he offered up a little prayer that it might be so.

Soon the two vessels were alongside, and after exchanging signals of recognition Waddell instructed the Sea King to follow him to a previously selected anchorage in the Porto Santo Bay on the north side of the nearby uninhabited islands known as Las Desertas, within sight of Madeira, where there was deep water and a smooth sea—an ideal location for the work in hand. Here the Sea King was anchored in seventeen fathoms, the Laurel came up and was lashed alongside her, and the work of transferring the supplies began without delay.

Tackles were quickly got aloft on both vessels, and all hands fell to work. Transferring the crates containing the big guns was the most difficult part of the job, and this was the first order of business. Hardly had the work begun when the main lift-fall gave way, and one of the big packing cases crashed down onto the deck, almost going overboard.

"Careful there, careful there," shrilled out Captain Ramsey in alarm. "For God's sake don't lose that piece of machinery!"

But there was no use in further dissembling. The force of the smashing fall had split the crate's boards apart, and an inquisitive member of the crew thrust his hand through the crack. Feeling the smooth

43

cylindrical surface of the big gun, he exclaimed, "Machinery! Yes, the same kind of machinery the Alabama carried! I know a 68-pounder when I lay my hand on it."

The news flashed electrically among the men, but they kept on working, and they only grinned when Ramsey kept calling out, "Easy with that glassware, men, don't let one of those barrels drop."

It was a tremendous task, but officers and men worked together without distinction of rank in their haste to get the job done, laboring without a letup from two o'clock in the afternoon until eleven o'clock at night when they stopped for a bite to eat. Then they started plugging away again by the light of the swaying lanterns hanging in the rigging, and kept at it until two the next morning, when they fell into their bunks dog-tired for a few hours' sleep. At daybreak they were at it once more, and by ten the last piece had been transferred, including the big, heavy iron safe in which was stored the sailing fund of golden British sovereigns, money that was legal tender in any part of the world.

Before the work of transferring the supplies was completed, Corbett and Waddell retired to the cabin of the Sea King and went through the official motions of transforming an East India merchantman into a Confederate cruiser. Corbett gave Waddell the bill of sale and formally turned the vessel over to him, retaining the register and other papers pertaining to the previous status of the ship, and Waddell promised that he would not commit any overt acts until Corbett had had time to get back to London and cancel the register. Waddell produced his commission as an officer of the Confederate States Navy and assumed command, and Corbett became a mere visitor on board.

The two men then went on deck and, as his last official act, Corbett ordered the boatswain to pipe all hands to the quarter-deck, where a round of grog was served. Then Corbett held up his hand for silence.

"Well, men," he said, "I have sold the ship to the Confederates. She is to belong to their navy, to be a cruiser, to burn and destroy merchant vessels. Of course you needn't go with her if you don't want to, but there will be a first-rate chance for any of you young men who will stop by the vessel, and I should advise you to do it."

But he was interrupted by murmurs and shouts of protest from some of the men.

"None of that for us!" they called out to Corbett. "Didn't you sign for Bombay? Do you call this making a Bombay voyage? Didn't you know this before you left London?"

Corbett was ready for that. He waved a copy of the ship's articles above his head.

"You signed these articles with me to go to Bombay or to any intermediate port, and if the ship were sold on the voyage you were to sign clear of her."

"We didn't hear anything about that in London."

"Well, here it is in the articles." Corbett read it to them in a firm voice. "And here's the new commander," indicating Waddell at his side. "Those of you who want to serve on the new cruiser, listen to what he has to say. Those who don't want to sign will be set ashore to be returned to London. But before you go I'll give you all another glass of grog, to show there's no hard feelings."

When the grog had been downed, Captain Waddell stepped forward, dressed in his brave new uniform of gray broadcloth, with two rings of gold braid on the cuffs and shining brass buttons bearing crossed anchors and the initials "C.S.N." He was a stout man of medium height, and he walked with a perceptible limp, the result of a wound in his left leg suffered in a youthful duel when he was serving as a midshipman in the old Navy. He was obviously ill at ease in his present unorthodox position and pulled nervously at the end of his moustache as he waited for the men to give him their attention. Then removing his gray cap, heavy with its wide band of gold braid, he stood during a moment of awkward silence, the wind stirring the thinning hair on his bare head.

"Men," he said, "I am an officer of the Confederate Navy, authorized to take command of this ship."

Here he offered to read his commission, but the men, livened up with the successive rounds of grog, shouted, "No, never mind that. Go ahead."

"Any of you that feel inclined to serve under the Confederate flag will get good wages and good treatment."

"And a nice salt water bath, like the men on the Alabama got," interrupted an irrepressible sailor.

"You needn't worry about that. I don't intend to fight. I intend to run away rather than fight. Anyone can see this vessel wasn't made to fight."

"No, you shipped those big guns just for ballast."
But Waddell went on.

"My orders are simply to destroy the Federal commerce by burning and destroying all ships that I can find sailing under the Federal flag. As each vessel is taken it will be valued and half the value of each will be divided among the ship's company and paid to them at the end of the war. I'm not asking you to sign for but six months. At the end of that time I'll either land you in a British port, or, if that's not possible, I will put you on a British ship bound for the United Kingdom. You will be fighting the fight of the oppressed against the oppressor, and you will receive good pay, all payment in gold."

"Hear! Hear!" they called. "Good pay? How much pay?"

Then the haggling started. The paymaster's desk had been prepared on the quarter-deck with a bucketful of bright gold sovereigns prominently displayed. The officers rattled the shining gold pieces with provocative ostentation, and another round of grog was served. But despite these inducements and despite the eloquence of Waddell's address, only a handful of the assembled sailors displayed any inclination to serve under the Confederate flag. Even these made it plain that they did not intend to sign up on the basis of the current scale of wages for ordinary seamen—about two pounds or less per month, but this difficulty had been anticipated and Waddell had been specifically authorized to pay higher wages than the prevailing scale and even to pay a bounty if necessary.

After long hours of bickering and dispute, interspersed with more rounds of grog, a total of twenty-three men were signed at varying scales of wages, determined partially by the seamanship of the men and partially by their skill in bargaining. Waddell was frankly disgusted at their mercenary attitude.

"They haggle about pay like a sharper! The modern sailor seems to have lost his recklessness and love of adventure."

But no amount of grumbling could dull the men's determination to drive as hard a bargain as they could. Waddell at first offered them what he thought was a very handsome proposition—four pounds per month and a bounty of fifteen pounds for signing the papers, but they turned up their noses at the offer. Somehow a rumor had spread through the ship's company that the new commander in the gray uniform was Admiral Semmes himself, and it was considered unlikely that the new cruiser's voyage would be a peaceful one if the notoriously aggressive Semmes was in command. At last, by dint of the most obstinate refusal to sign for less, the men brought Waddell's wage scale up to seven pounds a month and sixteen pounds bounty for ordinary seamen. Gunner's mates commanded fourteen pounds wages and twenty pounds bounty, and the ship's carpenter sixteen pounds and sixteen pounds bounty—all with two months' pay in advance.

On this basis the paymaster handed each of the new recruits his advance wages, and while they gloated over their handful of gold sovereigns, he wrote out the drafts for their bounty money and the allotments of pay to be sent home to their wives and dependents. Those who had declined service on the new cruiser were then directed to go on board the Laurel so that they could be sent back to England.

As the men gathered their luggage together and scrambled aboard the Laurel, Lieutenant Ramsey made no effort to conceal his vexation and disgust.

"I have never seen such a contemptible lot of curs in all my experience at sea."

Corbett himself came in for a good deal of criticism from both Ramsey and Waddell, who considered that he had not done all that he should have done to encourage the enlistment of his men in the Confederate service, and everybody was in a thoroughly bad humor when the time for departure came.

As soon as the transfer of the men had been effected, the Laurel got up steam, lifted her anchors, and cast off from the Shenandoah. But just at that moment, to everybody's alarm, a strange bark was discerned running down the island. The Shenandoah could not afford an encounter with an unfriendly vessel at this unpropitious moment, and the Laurel stood out to meet the stranger. The bark, however, ran up the British flag, the Laurel made a sweep around her for reassurance, and then went back to report to the Shenandoah that there was nothing to be feared, so the momentary flurry of excitement died down.

After taking on dispatches from the Shenandoah, the Laurel cast off again and, amid shouts of farewell, the two vessels parted forever. As the men on the Laurel looked back, they saw a strange new piece of bunting being hauled up to the cruiser's peak.

"It was a sort of a white flag," one of the men later testified, "with a blue cross up in the corner and a lot of stars—a right pretty flag." It was indeed a right pretty flag to the group of young officers gathered on the Shenandoah's deck, and as the Confederate ensign stiffened out in the breeze, a spontaneous cheer burst from their throats—a cheer in which the new recruits joined lustily. And why not? They were all loyal citizens of the Southern Confederacy now.

The Laurel went straight to Teneriffe in the Canaries where, after taking on coal, Ramsey sent Corbett and his men ashore, then struck out for Charleston, via Nassau. Corbett had fixed up a pretty cock-and-bull story for his men to tell, and told it himself to Mr. Dabney, the British consul. They were the survivors of the full-rigged British ship Sea King which had been wrecked and sunk off the coast of Madeira. There they had been rescued by the timely arrival of the Laurel, which had been kind enough to bring them to Teneriffe so that they could board one of the African mail ships and get back to England.

Mr. Dabney was at first inclined to accept this story at face value, but the tedium of waiting for a homeward bound ship was too much for the good behavior of the crew. Some of them drank a little too much rum and made the serious mistake of telling the truth. Thereupon the outraged consul put Corbett under arrest for violating the British neutrality laws, and when he boarded the mail ship Calabar with his crew for the return to London he found himself a prisoner.

Upon his return to England, Corbett was tried on the consul's charges, and although he was eventually acquitted on a technicality, the trial dragged out into the open all the details of the transactions involving the Laurel and the Sea King. Suspicions then were succeeded by facts, and a general world-wide alarm was sent out concerning the new Confederate raider. For the next twelve months the warships of the United States kept up a vigorous but fruitless search for her—in the Atlantic, in the Pacific, in the East Indies, in the West Indies, off the coast of Brazil— everywhere except where she was.

CHAPTER FIVE

A NEW SHIP AND A
GREEN CREW

———

WHEN THE SHENANDOAH hove up her anchor and stood out to sea under steam on the evening of October 20, she was a duly commissioned Confederate man-of-war. That is, she was a man-of-war technically speaking. As a matter of cold fact, she was still just a merchantman—a merchantman in hope of being transformed into a cruiser. Her guns lay in their cases on her decks, waiting to be mounted, and useless until they were. Kegs of powder and cases of shot and shell were piled helter-skelter in bewildering confusion on the deck, in the hold, wherever the loading crews had happened to dump them. Other supplies cluttered up her decks and passageways. Aside from the fact that she was now officially designated as such, she had none of the characteristics of a real warship.

Of her staff of officers, all except one were aboard her for the first time. Worst of all, she was pitifully and dangerously shorthanded. Twenty-three men was a hopelessly inadequate crew for a vessel the

size of the Shenandoah, a fact which was strikingly
impressed on Captain Waddell when he gave his first
order on his new command. Ordered to the break to
lift the anchor when preparing to cast off from Las
Desertas, the strength of the few available men
proved entirely unequal to the task. Their muscles
bulged, and sweat poured down their faces, but the
heavy anchor refused to budge from its muddy bed.
But the enthusiastic young officers, already initiated
into the process of working shoulder-to-shoulder with
the crew, did not hesitate when they saw the men
struggling helplessly at the winches. Quickly they
threw off their jackets and lent a hand. With their
assistance the anchor was lifted to the bow, and the
cruiser, as if inspired by this demonstration of co-
operation, sprang off to the southward on the first
leg of her momentous voyage.

The members of the crew were carefree and irre-
sponsible. They were sailors by profession, and it
made little difference to them what ship they were on
so long as they had a deck under their feet. The
young officers were full of the patriotism and the
invincible confidence of youth.

But sitting in his cabin, Captain Waddell was
weighed down with apprehension and a sense of his
responsibilites. Precipitated into the command of a
desperate and hazardous adventure, he brooded heavily over the problems, actual and potential, confront-
ing him. It was too much to be borne alone. He must
have somebody to talk to, so he sent for his young
chief officer, Lieutenant Whittle.

Whittle came to the captain's cabin and with some

difficulty found himself a seat in the crowded little
room, piled to the ceiling with kegs of powder temporarily stored there for safekeeping until a maga-
zine could be built.

"Mr. Whittle," the captain said gravely, "I want
to talk to you."

"Yes, sir," responded the chief officer, not knowing
what else to say and wondering just what was on the
commander's mind.

"This is my first command, you know," Waddell
began in his most dignified and formal manner.
"Naturally, I feel very keenly my responsibility to a
nation which is struggling for its very existence. I
am entrusted with an important cruise. You know
our objectives. Upon the accuracy of my judgment
in directing a voyage upon so vast a scale depends
success or failure. Success will be shared by every
individual under my command. But who will share
failure with me?"

This being obviously only a rhetorical question,
Whittle made no effort to supply the answer, and the
captain lumbered on ponderously with the unburden-
ing of his soul.

"And, I ask you, did ever a commander take over
a first command under more disadvantageous conditions? You know as well as I do that this vessel is a
cruiser in name only and can never be anything in
fact but a merchantman disguised as a man-of-war.
Somehow or other I hope to get her guns mounted so
that we may at least give other vessels a warlike impression. But I hope we may never be called on to
engage a real warship. And most certainly I hope we

shall not be brought to battle before we can add to this skeleton crew. We'd be wiped out if forced to fight now."

"Yes, we're shorthanded," agreed Whittle, "but even on short acquaintance, I like the looks of the officers. They seem a likely and willing bunch."

"I'm satisfied about the officers in spite of their inexperience," said Waddell. "They're all right. But I don't believe you've met them all yet because you weren't with us on the Laurel. Suppose I run over the list with you and tell you what I know about them— which isn't very much."

Opening his chest, he shuffled through the ship's papers to the register of officers.

"First," he began, "there are the lieutenants under you—John Grimball, Sidney Smith Lee, Jr., Dabney M. Scales and Francis T. Chew. Grimball's from South Carolina and a graduate of Annapolis. He's had experience on our ram Arkansas on the Mississippi and Yazoo rivers, and they tell me he's an expert at gunnery. Lee is from Virginia—"

"Lee of Virginia?" put in Whittle inquiringly. "Is he related to—"

"Yes," Waddell replied to the unfinished question, "he's Robert E. Lee's nephew. His father is Admiral Lee. This young fellow has not been to the Academy himself, but he's had a few years in the merchant service and he knows his way around a ship. He's a cheerful young cub, too. Full of jokes, and should be a good influence. I'm well impressed with him.

"Chew is a graduate of the Academy, but—you wouldn't believe it—he's never been to sea before. He's

55

been on some of our river gunboats, I believe, but he has a lot to learn about salt water sailing. Scales is a Mississippi man, an Academy graduate, and he served under Grimball on the Arkansas. He never has been to sea either, but Grimball speaks highly of him and I like the cut of his jib. I think he'll do all right as soon as he finds his sea legs.

"Our sailing master is Irving S. Bulloch—that rather dandified-looking young man with the side whiskers. He's from Georgia, a brother of Commander Bulloch in England. They say he's a skillful navigator."

"He was on the Alabama, wasn't he?" inquired Whittle.

"Yes, three of our officers were on the Alabama— Bulloch and Matt O'Brien, the chief engineer, and William Breedlove Smith, the paymaster. Smith's from Louisiana and seems efficient enough, but of course he's not a sailor—he's just a sea-going clerk. O'Brien is that big burly Irishman with the full beard. When he laughs you can hear him all over the ship, and he's always finding something to laugh about. Semmes rates him as one of the best engineers he ever saw, and everybody speaks of his wonderful disposition—always cheerful and keeping the men in good humor. Why, they tell me he kept up his joking on the Alabama when she was sinking until the water was actually lapping around his feet on the deck. He'll be a big help to us.

"We have a good man for surgeon—Dr. Charles E. Lining of South Carolina. He's thirty years old and an experienced naval surgeon. I hope we won't need him much, but we'll feel safer with him aboard. His assistant is Dr. Frank J. McNulty. He comes highly recommended.

"Our midshipmen are Orris A. Browne of Virginia and John T. Mason of Maryland. I don't know much about Browne, but Mason is a native of Maryland and he also served with Grimball on the Arkansas and later on Buchanan's flagship, the Baltic, in the defense of Mobile Bay. He knows what he's doing.

"The master's mates are Lodge Colton of Maryland and J. F. Minor and Cornelius E. Hunt of Virginia. They are likely looking lads—not much experience, but lots of enthusiasm and willing workers."

"Well," interrupted Whittle, "enthusiasm is a great thing, and I'm glad we have it on board, but we do seem to be a little short on experienced sea-going officers. What about the other men?"

"Don't worry about that," replied Waddell. "We have good men for all the key positions. O'Brien brought along his three assistants, all experienced in the British service—W. H. Codd, John Hutchinson, and Ernest McGuffeney. Henry Alcott, an old shellback, has shipped as sailmaker, and John L. Guy as chief gunner's mate. They're all Englishmen and thoroughly at home on a man-of-war. Some of them were on the Alabama, too. I'm not worried about them.

"In fact," he went on, "I'm not worried about any of the officers, although as you say they are mostly lacking in experience. That part of it's all right. But, Mr. Whittle, how can you hope to sail a ship of this size with a crew of twenty-three men? You're an experienced seaman. You know it can't be done."

Eager to calm the captain's anxiety, Lieutenant Whittle hastened to express a confidence which he did not entirely feel.

"We'll get plenty of recruits from the prizes we capture," he said. "Don't you worry about the crew. We'll be fully-manned before you know it and able to defend ourselves against any Yankee afloat. Meanwhile you can count on the officers for double duty. I've seen enough of these lads to know they'll do anything to help out without standing on ceremony."

"But that's not all," went on Waddell, improving the opportunity to pour out his apprehensions on sympathetic ears. "Think of my embarrassing political position. I'll make out somehow about sailing the ship. Managing a vessel in stormy weather is a science I have studied from boyhood. Fighting is a profession I have prepared myself for by study."

"I've heard my father speak in high praise of your reputation in the old Navy," Whittle reassured him.

"Yes, Mr. Whittle, I believe I am a good enough seaman to take care of my ship in any emergency. But here in command of the Shenandoah I am called on not only to sail and to fight but to be a politician and a diplomat as well—things I never learned on board a man-of-war. I shall have to decide on the high seas, impromptu, questions of international law which lawyers have quarreled over with all their books before them. I shall be forced to act promptly and without counsel, with little to guide me except my honor and my patriotism."

"He talks as though he were making a speech," thought Whittle to himself, disturbed at the commander's obvious nervousness. The prospective cruise promised to be hard enough at best. With a leader lacking in poise, it might easily be a failure. But he replied soothingly, to restore the captain's composure. "I'm sure you can handle everything all right."

"I've tried to prepare myself as well as I could," Waddell continued. "While I was waiting in Liverpool I studied the fundamental legal principles laid down by Blackstone. I have read Wheaton and Vattell on international law. Mr. Bulloch, I find, has thoughtfully placed Phillemore's *Laws of Nations* in my cabin. With these as a guide, I shall endeavor always to do what is right. And I shall, of course, rely on you and the other officers for your support."

"Feel free to call on me by all means whenever you think I can be of any help," said Whittle warmly. "But you'll get along all right. We'll soon have a full crew."

"I felt that I had to talk to somebody," the captain said, rather lamely as though suddenly ashamed of his jittery loquacity. "I trust you will understand."

"Quite so, sir." Whittle tried to agree heartily though he was himself a little upset by the commander's revelation of his uneasy frame of mind. "And now, sir, I suppose the first thing is to get the vessel ship-shape. I'm having the deck cleared so that we can get the guns mounted. I'd like you to come and see how well we are progressing."

And so they went above.

The purely physical problem of establishing some sort of order on board the ship was a monumental and staggering one. Captain Waddell had not magnified his difficulties. Transforming a merchantman into a man-of-war is a big enough task under the best conditions in a well equipped navy yard. To undertake such a conversion while under way at sea with an inadequate, untrained crew, facing the possibility of attack at any moment, was a task sufficient to daunt the most dauntless.

The first thing necessary was to get portholes cut and the guns mounted so that the vessel would at least have the appearance of a cruiser no matter what her actual capabilities as a fighting vessel might be. O'Shea, the carpenter who had come out on the Laurel, managed to find another man among the motley crew who knew how to handle a saw and hammer, and together they started the slow work of preparing to place the guns while the rest of the men fell to the task of clearing the jumbled stores from the deck.

But when the portholes had been cut in the side, the fighting bolts were nowhere to be found.

"I can't drive the damned bolts until I find them," complained O'Shea.

"Well, I'll find 'em if they're on the bloody ship," retorted Guy, the gunner.

Then started a raking of the vessel with a fine-tooth comb, searching for the missing bolts, but not until two days later were they accidentally located — in a beef barrel stored with the provisions in the hold! And that was but a sample of the confusion on board the ship. Next came the tackles for the guns, but they were not on board at all. Through some fatal oversight they had not been unloaded from the Laurel. There was, to be sure, plenty of rope on board, but there were no blocks suitable for gun tackles, and so the battery would be useless until tackles could be taken from a captured vessel.

Meanwhile the guns, in the absence of the fighting bolts and tackles, had been secured fore and aft, close to the ship's side. In place of the bolts, the guns were fastened to straps run through the scuppers and toggled outside the vessel. The decks gradually were cleared sufficiently for the men to walk around without stumbling over the miscellaneous boxes and crates with which they had been littered.

Then came the task of straightening out the stores, which in the confused haste of the transfer had been piled below decks regardless of their nature. Waddell, primarily a fighting seaman, thought first of the precious gunpowder. It had been stored temporarily in his and other officers' quarters, but after a few days a place was cleared for it in a small room directly under the captain's cabin—still in a vulnerable place above the waterline, but guarded with great caution against accident.

The officers worked cheerfully with the men on the fitting of the ship. While their cabins were used for temporary storage for powder and bread and vital perishables, they uncomplainingly bunked on the open decks and shared with the crew the informal toilet facilities afforded by the wash-deck buckets.

Even when they did gain access to their quarters they found accommodations of Spartan simplicity — seven cabins for ten officers, the furnishings consisting of a wash stand and bunk in each.

The middle-aged commander, accustomed for years to the trim comfort of well-kept officers' quarters, was outraged at the meagre furnishings of the captain's apartment.

"What a cabin!" he railed to Whittle. "Look at it! Look at that broken old plush-bottomed arm chair — my only piece of furniture! Smell of that carpet on the floor, stinking of dogs or something worse! No berth, no bureau, no lockers for my clothing, no washstand, no pitcher, no basin! Did ever a man-of-war's captain have such an apartment as this before? I'd like some of my shipmates in the old Navy to see this," and he laughed mirthlessly.

But the commander was game. After this outburst he endured his privations without further murmuring. While the work of fitting the ship was at its peak, with useful labor for every hand to do, he would limp forward and take the wheel himself so that another able-bodied seaman might be released for the emergency work. And though he spoke frankly to his chief officer of his qualms and apprehensions, he carried before his men an outer air of quiet confidence in the outcome of the cruise which helped to keep their spirits up.

Down the Atlantic they roared into the low latitudes. Only five of the men who had shipped at Las Desertas were found to be qualified for the engineer's department, and it was necessary to make a disposition of service between the deck hands and the black gang which would preserve health and good understanding. It was all-important to run the vessel as speedily as possible away from the neighborhood of the rendezvous to lessen the risk of pursuit and to seek lighter winds and a smoother sea for operations. Accordingly Captain Waddell had decided from the outset to keep the ship under steam during the daylight hours, and then, after nightfall, to stop the engines, put the vessel under sail, and change the course for the night. The wind was free, the course was to the southward, and as the breeze freshened after sunset, the ship logged nearly as much under sail as she did during the day under steam. The crew were seldom disturbed during the night, for the ship was kept under short canvas to prevent their being called from their rest.

Fortunately the builders of the ship had equipped her with the latest appliances for sailing, so that it was possible for even her limited crew to handle her efficiently. She was rigged with Cunningham's patent reefing topsails, with winches for lifting the topsail yards, and under sail, with a fair breeze, she had nothing to fear from any sailing vessel afloat.

Gradually the Shenandoah began to look more like what she purported to be. Her guns were useless until she could commandeer the necessary tackles, and the new-cut portholes yawned emptily. But for bringing-to her prospective victims she had available the two twelve-pounders which were part of the Sea King's original equipment, and as she neared the

Equator she began to keep a sharp lookout for enemy merchant vessels.

Lieutenant Chew had rigged himself a boatswain's seat and, letting himself down over the side, had painted out the name "Sea King." Thus, finally and formally, the East India merchantman passed out of existence. In her place there slid down the Atlantic the new-born Confederate cruiser Shenandoah, on the hunt for Yankee merchantmen unfortunate enough to cross her path.

CHAPTER SIX

THE FIRST PRIZE

E ARLY ON THE MORNING of October 27, for the
first time since leaving the Madeiras, the lookout in the crows-nest hailed the deck.

"Sail ho!"

"Whereaway?" the officer of the deck shouted the
stereotyped rejoinder, hastily scanning the horizon
in every direction.

"About two points off the lee bow, sir," the lookout cried down, "standing the same as we are."

"Can you make her out?"

"Aye, aye, sir; she's a square-rigged vessel. She's
a bark, with long mastheads. Looks like an American."

"Very good. Let me know when she shows her
colors."

Before the colloquy was ended, the whole ship's
company was in uproar. Officers and men swarmed
onto the deck and into the rigging for a look at the
stranger. Those fortunate enough to have glasses
passed them from hand to hand, and opinions about
the nationality of the strange bark passed wildly
about.

After about an hour it was possible to see that she flew the British ensign from her peak, but flying a British flag was a common protective device for Yankee merchantmen in those days, and as she looked thoroughly Yankee to Captain Waddell's practiced eye he determined to board her and have a look at her papers. So a blank cartridge from one of the twelve-pounders was fired across the bows of the surprised bark, and as she hove to an officer and boarding crew were dispatched in a small boat to ascertain her character.

To the disgust of the excited Confederates she proved upon examination to be the Mogul of London—American-built, but later sold to an English owner and now enjoying the protection of Her Majesty's flag. The captain of the Mogul had his wife and family on board with him, and Lieutenant Grimball, the boarding officer, a sentimentalist at heart, remarked privately that "they seemed so cosy and contented in their little home on the sea, I was half glad to find they were really entitled to the protection of the flag they flew and safe from capture." Most of those on board the cruiser, however, felt that they had been cheated of their rightful prey, and it was a glum and grumbling group that gathered that evening in the wardroom.

After this disappointing anticlimax followed three days of uneventful sailing, and then at nine o'clock in the morning of October 29 the warning cry rang again from the lookout's perch—and this time it was no false alarm. The first victim was about to fall to the Shenandoah.

It was the bark Alina from Searsport, Maine, bound for Buenos Aires with a cargo of railroad iron, and she was overhauled after a two hour's chase. The Alina, all unsuspecting of danger, innocently ran up the Stars and Stripes when signalled, and a gleeful prize crew with two officers was immediately sent aboard her.

Captain Staples of the Alina was a chapfallen skipper when he was informed that his bark was a prize of the Confederate States of America and he was ordered to get his papers and proceed on board the Shenandoah.

"I tell you what, matey," he grumbled to Hunt, the officer in charge of the boat that took him off to the cruiser, "I've a daughter at home that that craft yonder was named for, and it goes against me mightily to see her destroyed."

"Don't take it so hard," said Hunt soothingly. "I know how you feel, but it's just a matter of duty with us. There are plenty of civilians in the South that have to suffer too."

"I know," the captain admitted grudgingly. "I suppose I must take my chances with the rest. But," he flared up, "it's damned hard, it's damned hard, and I only hope I'll have a chance to return your polite attentions before this muss is over, that's all."

The Alina proved to be a most valuable and timely capture, for aboard her were found the blocks so sorely needed for the gun tackles, and there was also a supply of cotton canvas suitable for sail making. Captain Waddell salvaged a spring-bottomed mattress for his cabin, and the officers partially fitted themselves out with basins, pitchers, mess crockery, and knives and forks, most of which they had been doing without.

The Captain's navigating instruments were confiscated as legitimate spoils of war, but he and the other officers were permitted to go on board and bring off their clothing and such other personal property as they might wish to save. The members of the crew also were allowed to bring off all their baggage, which seemed to be more than they expected of their captors. They seemed inclined to treat the whole affair as a lark.

Having made his first capture, the next question facing Captain Waddell was the proper disposition of the prize vessel. Admiral Semmes at the outset of his career had attempted to take his prizes into neutral ports for adjudication, but the neutral nations held that this was not permissible, so Confederate raiders were forced to adopt the practice of destroying all the vessels they captured.

There were two methods open—scuttling or burning. Burning had the disadvantage of attracting too much attention, as the flames of a burning ship would be visible for thirty miles at night and would surely attract enemy war vessels if any were within that radius. In the case of a heavily laden vessel like the Alina scuttling was vastly preferable. It was quick and sure and left no trace. So O'Shea and his assistant were sent aboard with their augers, and soon they had riddled the bottom of the Yankee bark with a score of holes through which the water eagerly spurted.

The Alina was on her maiden voyage, thoroughly equipped, nicely coppered, and reported by the boarding crew to be spick-and-span throughout. Every seaman loves a beautiful ship, and the men of the Shenandoah shared the sorrow of the captive crew as they saw the trim vessel slowly settling. At length, about four o'clock in the afternoon, she suddenly settled by the stern, and the next minute there was nothing to be seen but a little eddy on the surface of the water where she had been. As one of the impressionable young officers set it down in his journal, "Her bows reared high in the air, as if in indignant deprecation of such sacrilegious treatment at the hands of seamen; and, with all sail set, she went down right bravely."

Midshipman Colton, hanging over the quarter railing, gulped as he saw her go down out of sight.

"I reckon it's all right," he said to Bulloch, who was standing by his side. "It's what we came out to do. But it's the first time I ever saw a vessel sink, and it makes me feel sick inside of me. It's too much like standing by a death-bed."

"Well, you've got to get used to it if you're going to serve on a raider," said Bulloch, whose service on the Alabama had hardened him to such sights. "That's what we're out for. The more we sink the better I'll like it."

While all this was going on, the crew of the Alina had been permitted to roam the decks of the cruiser while the men of the Shenandoah fraternized with them and with more or less subtlety suggested to them the advantages of becoming members of the

Confederate crew in preference to remaining on the vessel in the capacity of prisoners. Finally five seamen and a coal passer succumbed to the wiles of the volunteer recruiting officers and agreed to join. They were awarded the same bounty and scale of wages as those who had signed at Las Desertas and promptly assigned to their places of duty. The rest of the crew were confined in the top gallant forecastle, where they had ample time to reflect on the disadvantages of a prisoner as compared with a member of the crew, but after two days of this confinement (with no more enlistments) they were paroled and given the freedom of the ship.

The Alina's officers were paroled and accommodated in the limited hospitality of the ward room, where they were treated with such consideration that the captain admitted that he had little expected such kindness from an enemy. He remained disconsolate over the loss of the new bark named for his daughter, however, and refused all offers of liquor or invitations to join in the officers' conviviality. Finally he did thaw out sufficiently to join in the conversations, and soon he developed into a prize storyteller, narrating interminable yarns of his adventures on the high seas of the world. The callow young officers were delighted to have such an entertaining guest on board.

The capture of the Alina was a godsend to the Shenandoah in more ways than one. Not only did it supply them with the essential gun tackles and other much-needed supplies, but the additions to the crew came at a most opportune time. It served to lessen the burden of the overworked men who had shipped at Las Desertas, and now there was more leisure, more entertainment and frivolity. The men off duty would collect in the gangways and spend their time in singing, dancing, jumping, or in telling long stories—in all of which the narrator was always the hero. The tension of the first hard days of the voyage was relaxed.

Captain Waddell smiled as he observed the increasing good cheer of his men, and with no small degree of pleasure he entered in his log the notation of his first capture, valued at $95,000.

CHAPTER SEVEN

MORE VICTIMS

WITH THE ALINA as an appetizer, the Shenandoah now entered upon a busy week of destruction, during the course of which no less than six unwary Yankee merchant vessels fell victims to the Confederate raider.

It was on November 5 that the schooner Charter Oak of Boston was chased, captured, and burned. She was a small vessel, valued at $15,000, with a crew consisting of only a mate and three swarthy Portuguese sailors beside the captain. When the Portuguese were brought on board the cruiser and their baggage was examined, it was found that they all had blue army overcoats, and a strict examination brought out the fact that they were all deserters from the Federal army—members of that tribe known contemptuously as bounty jumpers.

The master of the Charter Oak, Captain Samuel J. Gilman, took his capture philosophically enough. When Waddell pushed off to examine the little schooner before burning her, Gilman shouted after him, "For God's sake bring back the preserved fruit you'll find in the cabin. You're probably not carrying much dessert aboard the cruiser."

The Shenandoah's men did not fail to heed. They

brought aboard not only the preserved fruit and other delicacies they found in the cabin larder, but also the two thousand pounds of canned tomatoes and other vegetables which constituted part of the Charter Oak's cargo. Captain Waddell also found a sword in the schooner's cabin, which he picked up and brought along.

"You can't tell. We might find some need for it," he said musingly to Whittle.

There was a mild flutter of excitement when Captain Gilman informed his captors that he was carrying a good supply of a rare and highly desirable commodity—ice! There were several hundred pounds of it, he told them, packed in sawdust in a big hogshead in the hold, and the thirsty young officers had entrancing visions of the cooling drinks they were going to have with Captain Gilman's ice tinkling pleasantly in the frosted glasses. So the hogshead was sought out and painstakingly lowered into one of the cruiser's boats, where it made an awkward and unmanageable cargo. In rounding the Shenandoah's stern on the return trip the top-heavy boat almost capsized, the propeller shaft was fouled, and two of the sailors were thrown overboard and almost drowned before they could be fished out of the water. But at length the hogshead was laboriously hoisted on deck and its head was eagerly stove in. With parched tongues the sailors gathered expectantly to get a first glimpse of the precious ice—and then came the shattering anticlimax. The hogshead was full of sawdust and water. Under the tropic sun, despite its protective insulation, the priceless ice had melted.

In time the Shenandoah's crew were to have on deck more ice than they knew what to do with, but never again was there such a letdown as the heartbreaking discovery of the hogshead's contents.

The capture of the Charter Oak was an event of special interest because it provided the Shenandoah with her first feminine passengers. The little schooner's cruise, it seemed, was a sort of family affair. Captain Gilman had brought along with him not only his wife but also his wife's red-headed sister, Mrs. Gage, and her four-year-old son. Mrs. Gage was a buxom widow, her husband, a sergeant in the Federal army, having lost his life in the fighting at Harper's Ferry. All of them were permitted to bring their personal effects off the schooner before she was burned, and Captain Waddell turned over to the family party his own starboard cabin for their quarters.

Waddell was greatly embarrassed by the necessity of having to entertain the ladies as unwilling guests on board his vessel, and was determined to do everything possible to make them feel at their ease. He had taken from the schooner's cabin the ship's money, $200 in gold, and this he turned over to Mrs. Gilman, very formally in the presence of Midshipman Mason, as a gift from the Southern Confederacy.

To Mason he explained apologetically, "I feel a compassion for these poor women. They will be landed I don't know where. It's hard on them. The least I can do is give her back her husband's money."

Captain Gilman was surprised and at first pleased to find another Yankee skipper on board the Shenandoah; but he and Captain Staples, although both down-Easters, did not hit it off together very well. As the Charter Oak went up in flames, Gilman asked Staples, as one sufferer to another, "What did he do to you?"

"He scuttled me," the Alina's master answered sourly. But Gilman only laughed.

The Charter Oak carried a light cargo, making scuttling impracticable, so it was necessary to burn her Accordingly, after her valuables had been removed, all the tar, pitch, and turpentine on board were sprinkled over the vessel, the bulkheads were chopped down and piled up in her cabins and forecastle, all hatches were opened, and all halyards let go so that the sails might hang loosely, and the yards were counter-braced. Fire was then taken from the galley, and within a few minutes she was roaring with flame. To make sure that she was completely destroyed, Captain Waddell determined to remain near her for a few hours after nightfall. To guard against surprise, he ran to leeward of the burning wreck.

"If a Yankee cruiser is in this neighborhood and is attracted by the flames," he explained to the officer of the deck, "she will most likely be under sail. If she is to leeward, she could not work up fast enough to investigate the fire. With steam, she would run to windward to get a look, and that would give us the advantage of seeing her first. We'll be safe here."

The sight of the burning ship was a novel one to most of those on board the cruiser, and, fascinated by the lurid spectacle, they watched intently until the last red ember dropped hissing into the quiet sea.

"I never saw anything like that before," breathed the deeply impressed Lieutenant Scales.

"We burnt up fifty like that when I was on the Alabama," returned Bulloch, with all the lofty superiority to which his service on the famous raider entitled him. "You've got to get used to it."

The day after the capture of the Charter Oak was the first Sunday of leisure aboard the new cruiser. In the morning the crew was mustered on the poop deck and Whittle read them the articles of war. There was some murmuring among the crew as they learned of the numerous offenses for which the punishment of death was prescribed. Some of them realized for the first time that being on board a man-of-war was serious business.

At about eleven o'clock on the morning of the eighth the lookout on the fore-topsail yard reported a sail in sight, and, as there was only a light breeze stirring, the cruiser got up steam and proceeded to overhaul the stranger. When boarded by Bulloch, Scales and Hunt, she proved to be the bark D. Godfrey from Boston, bound for Valparaiso with a cargo of lumber, salt beef, and pork. The salt meat was much needed by the cruiser, and twenty-two barrels were removed to the Shenandoah before the bark was condemned to destruction by fire.

Darkness had settled down by the time the bark was well ablaze, and the flames which licked up the sails and rigging made a light so brilliant that every burning rope could be plainly seen in flaming silhouette against the blackness of the tropical night.

Soon the yards came thundering down as the lifts and halyards were burned through. The standing rigging parted like blazing threads, and the spars simultaneously went by the board and left the hulk wrapped from stem to stern in one fierce blaze like a floating furnace.

As the Shenandoah stood by and watched the fire, Captain Hallett, the late commander of the Godfrey, tramped up and down the cruiser's quarter-deck in a sad and bitter mood.

"That was a vessel that did her duty well for forty years," he said to one of the Confederate officers. "She has faced all kinds of weather in every part of the world. And, after such a career, to be destroyed by men's hands deliberately on a calm night on this tropical sea is too bad."

"It's just one of the results of this terrible war," volunteered Mrs. Gilman, who stood gloomily watching the burning ship. "I wish to God it was over!"

"Yes, terrible," the captain of the Godfrey agreed. "It's bad enough on land, where at least you've a solid foundation under you; but it's worst of all at sea, where it destroys the few planks that you have learned to trust. There was never a sight so awful to a sailor as a ship on fire. It tears the heart out of you, even when you know that there's no human being on board—but I suppose there's nothing to be gained by grumbling." He shrugged his shoulders resignedly.

The capture of the Godfrey not only furnished the cruiser with a supply of meat, but also provided five new members for the crew. On this day

also one of the crew of the Alina belatedly decided
to cast his lot with the Confederates, and was transferred from the prisoners' brig to the crew list.

Some of the members of the crews of the Shenandoah's victims, after it was all over, voiced the
complaint that their enlistment with the cruiser was
not entirely a matter of free will. The use of what
they called "rough persuasion" was charged. They
were forced to work by day, they said, and then put
in irons at night. Not only put in irons, they complained, but crowded into the topgallant forecastle
with the sheep and the hens!

"A beastly unpleasant experience," one of them
testified—probably no over-statement of the truth.

One of those who joined the man-of-war's crew
from the Godfrey was the cook, John Williams, a
free negro. Williams was a veteran of the United
States Navy, having served on board the Congress
and on the Minnesota, and he had spunkily told
Bulloch, who headed the boarding crew, that if the
Minnesota were there she would blow the Shenandoah
out of the water.

"Yes, but she's not here," retorted Bulloch with
crushing simplicity, and the cook went muttering
glumly back to his pots and pans.

Aided by the new members of the crew, Captain
Waddell was able to get all the guns in position. The
deck was of soft pine and only four inches thick,
so the engineers fastened iron plates to the decking
to strengthen it, and the train tackles of the gun
carriages were hooked to these plates. Now, at last,

the Shenandoah was a cruiser in fact as well as in name. With her guns in place and with men on board to man them, she was now ready to take her chances against all comers. Captain Waddell slept more soundly that night.

By this time the ship, with forty prisoners on board, was becoming crowded, with far too many passengers for the comfort and safety of the crew. But the next day a passing Danish brig, the Anna Jane, was hailed, and Waddell dickered with the Danish master to take aboard eight of the prisoners and set them ashore at the nearest port, Rio de Janeiro. After some bargaining, the Dane accepted a chronometer, a barrel of beef, and a barrel of ship biscuits as his fee, and so the transfer was made. With Captain Staples, who went aboard the Anna Jane with the chronometer of the Alina which was used in the transaction, were Captain Hallett and the mates and two men each from the Alina and the Godfrey.

Captain Gilman objected to being sent off on the Anna Jane with his family and crew, raising the issue that when they got to Rio they would still face the problem of getting back to their home in California. Captain Waddell obligingly agreed to continue to hold them prisoners on the cruiser in the hope of being able to put them on board some vessel bound for the Golden Gate. Dr. Lining was disturbed at Waddell's softness.

"They are so comfortable they don't want to leave," he told Lieutenant Whittle. "The Captain should have made them go along with the others."

On the other hand, Lining strongly questioned the wisdom of sending any of the prisoners ashore so soon, fearing that they would spread the news of the Shenandoah's whereabouts and bring down the Yankee cruisers on her track. But Waddell asked nobody's advice about the matter, and Captain Gilman settled down contentedly on board, smoking his pipe and regaling the young officers with long and highly colored yarns of his experiences at sea and with the Digger Indians in California.

The next day the lookout sighted the brig Susan of New York, out of Cardiff with a cargo of coal bound for the Rio Grande.

"She looks like a steamer!" reported the deck officer with a troubled frown as soon as he was able to get a view of her with his glass. "She's moving slowly, but there's no sign of smoke."

This was disconcerting to Captain Waddell. A steamer would most likely be a Yankee cruiser. With an anxious eye he scrutinized the brig as her visibility increased.

"What is that contraption on her side?" he asked, puzzled, when at last he got a good view of her. "It looks like a paddle wheel, but it isn't a wheel. Let's have a closer look at her."

So the gunner fired a blank shell, the brig hove to, and the boarding crew set off under Chew and Browne.

The Susan turned out to be a *rara avis* of the sea. Her master, Captain Hansen, was a German Jew. The brig was very old and very weak, and such a sluggish sailer that the barnacles grew to her bottom as she crept along. Furthermore she leaked at every seam, leaked so badly that the water poured in faster than the crew could possibly pump it out. Accordingly Captain Hansen had devised an ingenious machine—simple, but useful only in a breeze—by means of which she was kept afloat.

To the pump was attached a shaft half the beam of the vessel in length, and on the outer end of this shaft was placed a paddle wheel, giving her the appearance of a steamer. The purpose of the wheel, however, was to turn the pump, and the quantity of water discharged from the hold by this crude device depended upon the velocity of the hull through the water, which was never very great. But it was superior to man-power alone, and by means of it the Susan had been able to keep from sinking.

"What a miserable tub!" exclaimed Captain Waddell contemptuously. "I almost believe that Captain Hansen is glad he fell in with us. He's probably got her well insured, and it's a good business deal for him."

Waddell's contempt was heightened when Hansen offered to renounce his allegiance to the United States and join the Shenandoah if given an appointment as an acting master's mate, but the cruiser needed enlisted men rather than officers, so Hansen had to be rated as a paroled prisoner. He accepted this without comment, and sat on the poop unconcernedly smoking his pipe as the Susan was scuttled and went heavily to the bottom. There was little booty on the Susan, but Smith Lee found a dog on board which he promptly adopted as his own and took aboard the Shenandoah as the official mascot of the ship.

The sun was just going down on the eleventh when a sail was discovered to the south and east on the port tack, standing to the south and west. In spite of the quick-falling tropical darkness, the Shenandoah immediately set off in the first night chase of her career.

There was lively discussion on board as to whether it would be possible to overhaul the intended victim in the dark. Some of the more pessimistic doubted openly whether they would ever come up with her.

"You may be lucky if you don't," darkly commented Captain Hansen, who was taking a lively interest in the proceedings. "She may be one of our cruisers—and then you'll wish you'd never seen her."

But Captain Waddell deigned no reply to the dire prophecy of the prisoner. He merely sniffed, and remarked in a dignified but audible aside to Whittle, "Pay no attention to the old reprobate. There are croakers to be found in every class of society."

A few minutes after midnight came the lookout's cry of "Sail ho!" Soon there rose up out of the darkness a fine large clipper of 1,100 tons. Lieutenant Lee headed the boarding party, and he found her to be the Kate Prince of Portsmouth, New Hampshire, Captain Henry Libbey, with a cargo of coal. Lee also reported that the entire crew of twenty-one men expressed a desire to join the Shenandoah, and that the captain's wife boldly declared herself a Southern sympathizer and said she would enjoy nothing better than sailing aboard the Confederate raider.

Waddell was reluctant to miss such an opportunity

to recruit his crew up to something like an effective
force, but he already had too many prisoners—certainly too many women on board—so he ransomed the
Kate Prince for $40,000, and put all his remaining
prisoners on board her to be set ashore at her first
port. There were Captain Gilman and his wife, Mrs.
Gage and her little boy, C. Bearse the second mate,
F. Rocas the steward, T. Burgess, J. M. Sampson,
J. Monroe, T. Eanis—all of the Charter Oak; and
Captain Hansen, H. Payne the mate, C. Henschell
the second mate, and W. Dunn the steward—all of
the Susan. Gilman and his wife protested against
the transfer, intimating that Waddell was guilty of a
breach of faith in not keeping them aboard. By dint
of courteous persuasion, however, Waddell at length
induced them to accept their freedon.

The Kate Prince, with her load of refugees, landed
at Pernambuco on November 29, and the United
States consul there immediately notified Adams in
London and Seward in Washington. The prisoners
gave a minutely detailed technical description of the
Shenandoah, and an immediate warning was sent out
to all United States cruisers to be on the lookout for
her.

The "lady prisoners," as Captain Waddell politely
called them, gave a glowing account of the chivalrous
treatment accorded them by the Rebel pirates, and
back on the Shenandoah the frivolous young officers
thenceforth always referred to the captain's starboard cabin as "the ladies' cabin."

Late in the afternoon of the eleventh the cruiser
chased and stopped the bark Adelaide, showing the

flag of Buenos Aires, and thereupon ensued one of the most involved and puzzling legal complications encountered in the Shenandoah's whole voyage. Captain Williams, upon being questioned, stated that he was bound from New York to Rio with a cargo of flour. The cargo, he said, belonged to Phipps & Company of New York and the ship to a Mr. Pendergast of Baltimore, described as "a good Southerner." The bark's real name was the Adelaide Pendergast, but Captain Williams declared that Pendergast had changed her name and transferred her registry to the Buenos Aires colors in order to save his property from the hated Yankees. Captain Waddell was a stickler for the legal proprieties, but all this sounded so untrustworthy to him that he decided to burn the vessel and let the Confederate government settle with Pendergast. Accordingly orders were given to bring aboard the Shenandoah all the hams, preserved fruit, and other provisions in the Adelaide and then prepare her for the torch.

While this was being done, Lieutenant Bulloch found in the cabin a bunch of letters which proved that both ship and cargo belonged to the "good Southerner" Pendergast, and that the name of Phipps & Company had been used merely to give a good Yankee disguise to the cargo. When these letters were brought to Waddell he instantly reversed his decision and ordered all the plunder returned to the Adelaide. Some damage had already been done to the ship and cargo in preparing for her burning, and Captain Waddell wrote Pendergast a polite letter of apology for this damage. By way of further amends,

Captain Williams was presented with a barrel of sugar, and also a barrel of lamp oil to replace that which had been poured over the cargo of flour in preparing to burn it. At the last minute it occurred to the painstaking Waddell that the Yankees might have their suspicions aroused by this strange sparing of Pendergast's bark and that harm might thereby come to that Confederate-minded Marylander. Accordingly Waddell formally bonded the cargo, while admitting the ship to be neutral—thus compounding a duplex misrepresentation of the facts. But Waddell's sense of propriety was satisfied by the complicated subterfuge, and the Adelaide went happily on her way, content to be spared by whatever device.

Two days later, on Sunday the thirteenth, the ship's second muster was held, and this time the crew, as well as the officers, were dressed in their regulation Confederate gray uniforms. Before the muster was completed a sail was sighted which proved to be a little New England schooner, the Lizzie M. Stacey out of Boston, bound for the Sandwich Islands by way of Cape Horn. She was brand-new, and such a splendid little sailer that it took several hours to overtake her, but at last she was forced to pull up and submit to the inevitable boarding crew.

As the schooner's master, Captain Archer, came on board the Shenandoah, Whittle spoke out in sincere admiration.

"My congratulations to you, Captain! Nobody but an American skipper would have the hardihood to venture halfway around the world in a little craft like that."

But the grumpy old captain was in no mood for pleasantries.

"It's nothing," he growled. "We thought nothing of such sailing in the old days. But damn if there ain't the most lubberly set of sailors afloat in these latitudes I ever fell in with. Day before yesterday I ran across the bows of a big English ship bound to Australia, and blast me if all hands didn't make a rush forward to see me as though I'd been the sea serpent or some other almighty curiosity."

"Yes," chimed in his Irish mate, "they invited us to come on board for a visit with them—"

"But I'd no time for visiting," went on the captain. "There was a stout breeze blowing at the time, and I'd no notion of losing a good run just for the sake of showing off a little before a lot of lubbers who seem to think that nothing less than a seventy-four is safe to cross the ocean in. But I suppose if we'd wasted a little time with the lubbers, maybe we'd have missed the pleasure of meeting you today, Mr. Rebel." From the standpoint of size and value, the Lizzie M. Stacey was not much of a prize, but she was Yankee-owned and flew the Yankee flag, and so she was burned.

CHAPTER EIGHT

ACROSS THE LINE

THE SHENANDOAH's busy week had been spent in the low latitudes of the North Atlantic where the tracks of outward bound vessels cross. The Lizzie M. Stacey had been captured in 1° 43′ north latitude. Now, as the cruiser turned her course southward to speed on her way to her ultimate destination in the North Pacific, there loomed ahead of the crew the elaborate ceremonies always incident to the crossing of the Equator.

Even on a lone Confederate raider matching her wits against the searching cruisers of the whole United States Navy, every sailor—officer or enlisted man—when he makes his first crossing of that imaginary line must make the acquaintance of Father Neptune and his court; and Captain Waddell, though weighed down by worries and anxious to get along as rapidly as possible, was the kind of man who would never think of permitting business to interfere with this traditional frivolity.

Mischief-loving Smith Lee was among the foremost planners of the ceremony in which a few hapless members of the crew were introduced to His Marine

Majesty. Officers and men alike were led before King Neptune for absolution and baptism. Tar and grease were applied to the unfortunates, the barrel-hoop razor was wielded with no regard for the sensibilities of the victims, and the final baptismal ceremonies were effected in a shallow tank improvised from a tarpaulin, fed by a chilling stream of salt water from a two-inch fire hose.

Not satisfied with the initiation of all the legitimate victims of their buffoonery, the men in their mounting enthusiasm seized on the luckless sailmaker, Henry Alcott, who was regarded on board as "an odd character," and dragged him kicking to the quarter-deck where Neptune had established his court. When Alcott offered to fight they only howled the merrier, and picked him up with mock sympathy as the stream from the fire hose knocked him off his feet.

The Equatorial celebration behind them, the officers and men settled down to their serious business. With a cracking southeast trade wind, the ship with all sail set ran southward off the coast of Brazil. The weather was delightful, and expectations were entertained of falling in with some of the Yankee clippers bound from San Francisco to New York around the Horn. To their surprise and disappointment, however, there ensued a period of several days during which no enemy vessels were encountered, and the men on board had ample time to devote to their own amusement.

Fortunately for their entertainment, the former owners of the Sea King had equipped her with an excellent library of more than six hundred volumes, and during their abundant leisure the young officers found refuge in reading, playing chess and cards, swapping yarns, and speculating what the future might hold in store for them.

There also began to crop out cautious questions as to the ability and capacity of the skipper. Before they had left England it had been whispered that some of the older Confederate naval officers were not entirely satisfied with Waddell's selection. Was he the man for the job? There were only the vaguest murmurings, but there was a visible shadow of discontent in the wardroom.

Lookouts, of course, were kept aloft night and day, and the crew were kept busy putting things aboard the cruiser shipshape. When all the emergency work had been done, there were still a few odd jobs of tidying up. The ship's bell was dismounted and taken below to the engine room to have the name "Sea King" filed off. A grindstone was brought on deck, and the name of the vessel was ground off the wheel, one of the prisoners from the Lizzie M. Stacey being given the privilege of turning the grindstone.

From time to time there would be a flurry of excitement as the lookouts spied a sail, but it always proved to be of British or other neutral registry. It was not until December 4, when they had reached latitude 37° 47′ south, fifty miles southeast of Tristan d'Acunha, that a craft was discovered which had the general appearance of an American. Upon investigation, however, she turned out to be the Sardinian Ship Dea del Mare, from Genoa to Rangoon, and the Shenandoah passed herself off as the U. S. S.

De Soto on a cruise looking for Confederate raiders.

On the same day, when the Italian had hardly been lost to sight, another sail was seen, and this, when it came into plain view, was pronounced by one of the old sea-dogs of the crew to be unmistakably an American whaler. She was a bluff-bowed, square-sterned, old fashioned craft—the Edward from New Bedford —of about 400 tons, and had been whaling for nearly fifty years. She had been out of New Bedford for four months and had taken but one right whale. The cruiser came upon her while she was engaged in the process of butchering the whale and hoisting the huge pieces on board for boiling out the blubber. So busily were the whaler's crew engaged in this work that the cruiser came within easy range of her before being observed.

Captain Charles P. Worth, of the Edward, accepted the adverse fortunes of war in rare good humor, and when brought on board the Shenandoah he courteously greeted the assembled officers.

"Good afternoon, gentlemen. You have a fine ship here for a cruiser."

"Yes, sir," responded Lieutenant Mason, the officer of the deck, "and that vessel of yours looks as if she was familiar with salt water."

"She was laid on the stocks before you and I were born," Captain Worth agreed, and then, leaning nonchalantly on the rail, he fell into an easy and affable conversation with Mason about whales and whaling, concealing the regret and sorrow he felt at the loss of the old ship of which he had been master for nearly twenty-five years.

Bulloch and Minor were sent aboard the Edward to take charge of her for the night, the crew meanwhile being transferred to the Shenandoah and put in irons for safety's sake.

The most gratifying thing about the capture was the opportunity it afforded for replenishing the Shenandoah's depleted stores. Whalers are generally better provisioned than most vessels, and the Edward proved no exception. The cruiser lay alongside her for two days supplying her larder with 100 barrels of beef and as many of pork, 800 pounds of sugar, 7,000 pounds of ship's biscuit ("the best I have ever seen," said Waddell), four chests of tea amounting to 180 pounds, butter, coffee, tobacco, soap, and a quantity of whale line, cotton canvas, blocks, and other tackle. Two of her five boats were new, so these replaced two of the old and worthless ones of the Shenandoah in the davits, the other three being lashed astern for future emergencies.

Before they had completed the task of transferring the plunder, a sail was sighted. Leaving a prize crew on the Edward, the Shenandoah set out under steam in pursuit of the stranger. The chase had hardly begun before a quick squall of rain came up, obscuring the quarry. This was somewhat embarassing, as nobody on board had taken her bearings and it was necessary to proceed purely by guess, which Waddell did. Whittle and Grimball, backed up by Dr. Lining, thought the captain was heading far astern of her and so expressed themselves. Waddell, however, said he was confident he was on the right course and went ahead. After about a half hour the squall passed, and the pursued ship loomed up broad off on the cruiser's bow—just about where the junior officers had said she would be. The young men could not conceal their elation over this vindication of their judgment—and the captain made no effort to conceal his chagrin.

"I would have given a great deal to be right about it," he told Lining plaintively, "you young fellows seem so rejoiced over my mistake."

"We are not rejoicing to find you wrong," Lining assured him, "but are merely pleased that we were right. Everybody likes to be right, you know; it's human nature."

There was no further discussion of the subject, but the episode did not serve to improve relations between the captain and his officers. The ship, when over-taken, proved to be an Engish craft, so the cruiser returned to the Edward and resumed the work of transferring the stores.

When this task was completed, and all the officers had satisfied their curiosity by visiting the whaler on a sightseeing trip, the Shenandoah steamed off for the settlement on the northwest side of Tristan d'Acunha for the purpose of landing her prisoners there. Early the following morning the mountainous island loomed ahead of them, and soon it was possible to make out the British flag flying at the flagpole in the settlement. Hardly had the Shenandoah come into view before a boat put off from the shore, and as soon as she came closer it was seen that she was loaded with milk, eggs, chickens, and fresh meat— just what the cruiser most needed.

The islands were officially a British possession, but

the twenty-six residents were mostly castaways and derelicts of sundry nationalities. One of them, a native of Connecticut, by virtue of being the oldest inhabitant, called himself the head man. He was astonished when he saw the Confederate ensign fluttering from the man-of-war's peak, and even more surprised when told that the cruiser had thirty-five prisoners it intended to land there.

"And where did you get any prisoners?" inquired the mystified head man.

"From a New Bedford whaler, not far from here," responded one of the officers.

"And what became of the whaler?"

"We burned her up."

"Hell!" exclaimed the one-time Yankee. "Is that what you do to the ships you capture?"

"Yes, if they belong to the United States. We're in a war, you know."

"All right," agreed the head man with a dubious shake of his head. "You know your own business, I guess. But my notion is that this sort of pranks will get you into the devil's own muss before you are through with it. What your quarrel is with the United States I don't know, but I'm damned if I believe they'll stand this kind of work."

One of the expatriate Yankees on the islands, however, expressed his own opinion that the South was in the right and would eventually triumph, but as he immediately struck up a negotiation for the sale of a quantity of fresh beef, there arose some question about the genuineness of his sympathy. There was, however, no questioning the desirability of his fresh meat, so a trade was soon made with him, irrespective of his political views, taking his meat at eight cents a pound and paying for it with flour at seven dollars a barrel. Waddell also bought milk, sheep, pigs, and geese.

Meanwhile the crew of the Edward, mostly natives of the Sandwich Islands, and the remaining prisoners on board were being set ashore with their luggage, together with sufficient provisions to keep them from suffering until they could be picked up—1,680 pounds of bread, four barrels of pork, and four of beef. Captain Worth and Captain Archer were among those set ashore here, and in appreciation of his good sportsmanship, Captain Worth was given back his quadrant, spyglass, navigation books and epitome, and also presented with sixty pounds of tobacco, two boxes of coffee, one of soap, and a supply of medicine. It was with genuine regret that the Shenandoah's officers parted with Captain Worth. Brave and open-hearted, he had inspired them all with respect.

It was a source of regret to all that the exigencies of the occasion made it necessary to leave the prisoners on this rather out-of-the-way island. It was indeed a regular port of call for some ships, but it might be months before they could be picked up and carried home. Captain Waddell, not yet calloused to the infliction of the hardships of war, worried over this no little, but he might have spared himself, for the marooned men were rescued within three weeks. The United States warship Iroquois, cruising the South Atlantic in feverish search of the Shenandoah, touched at Tristan d'Acunha on December 28, and Captain Worth and the others were taken on board the warship and carried to Cape Town. Commander Rogers of the Iroquois duly reported the rescue to Secretary Welles at Washington and enclosed with his report a detailed description of the Rebel raider obtained from the careful nautical observations of Captains Worth and Archer.

This description of the Shenandoah, as furnished by the two Yankee captains, is a masterpiece of photographic accuracy and stands as a monument to their powers of close observation while confined aboard her. A skilled naval architect might almost build the ship from these specifications:

"Length, 230 feet; beam, 32 feet; tonnage, about 1,100. Three masts, ship-rigged, carrying three royals, no crossjack.

"Dogvane on each mast (arrows) and conductors on all masts. Lower masts and topmasts of iron; lower and topsail yards of iron. Rolling topsails, wire rigging, set up inside, but has chain plates and channels.

"Smokestack abaft the mainmast, and close to it (within ten feet). Telescopic smokestack; escape pipe forward of smokestack. One ventilator on each side of the smokestack and two on poop deck, of brass. Break of poop deck extends forward of the mizzenmast about ten feet. Large wheelhouse, about nine feet high, with rounded roof on poop deck, abaft the mizzenmast (of teak wood). Short bowsprit, with ordinary steeve; a rather straighter stem than usual; jib and flying jib-boom in one. All standing rigging and all brace and staysail pendants of wire rope. Carries two boats on a side. Waist boats swing on high iron davits, halfway between fore and main masts. Quarter boats the same, between mizzenmast and smokestack. Carries a boat across topgallant forecastle. Carries two large boats on house between fore and main masts. Break of topgallant forecastle a little forward of foremast. A big chafe on port side, abreast of fore-rigging, low down. No poles about eyes of royal rigging. Doublings of masts quite long; outriggers at topmast crosstrees for topgallant backstays. Top of monkey rail on main deck much lower than the poop deck. No rake to the masts.

"Pierced for eight guns, four on a side; no pivots. Abaft the break of the topgallant forecastle, one 32-pounder on each side (Whitworth muzzle-loading rifles). Next, abaft in the waist, two 7-inch guns on each side, ordinary smooth-bores. Just forward of break of poop, two small guns (probably 8-pounders).

"Had aboard seventy-four persons, all told. Officers stated that her greatest speed was, under steam, 13 knots; under sail, 15 knots. Carries main and mizzen trysail gaffs, stationary aloft, with chain spans. No studding-sail booms, and no boom irons on lower yards. Double topping lifts to the spanker boom, wire rope. Spanker boom projecting some distance beyond the taffrail. Mizzen stays set up on each side of smokestack, in the deck. A house on main deck from bridge to foremast. Compass on house forward of bridge. Bridge halfway between main and

fore masts. Boxes for sidelights on each side of
bridge.

"General appearance is that of a long, narrow
ship, quite taut, and with quite square yards. Has
six cabin windows (quite large) in the round of her
stern. Figurehead, large figure of a man standing
upright, with one arm broken off. Smokestack parallel to the mainmast. Carved work on stern, painted
white. Her propeller hoists up.

"Rounded stern, rather full. No trysail masts.
Brace pendants on lower and topsail yards.

"Measurements are all by the eye, and only ap-
proximate."

CHAPTER NINE

AROUND THE CAPE

LEAVING TRISTAN D'ACUNHA, the Shenandoah struck out to the eastward. To make use of the belt of strong westerly winds which circles the globe south of the forty-third parallel, she was headed slightly to the southward from the latitude of the island, and to save coal she was put under canvas and her propeller triced up.

While engineer O'Brien was securing the lifted propeller, he suddenly saw something that made his blue Irish eyes bulge in their sockets. There, entirely across the face of the brass band which went around the coupling of the shaft, was a long, wicked-looking crack—just a little crack, but a dangerous menace to the success of the expedition. When the news of the disconcerting discovery was conveyed to Captain Waddell he was filled with consternation. It was possible to patch it up temporarily for emergency use, but he felt that no reliance was to be placed in any such makeshift repair job. If anything was certain it was that a steamship was no stronger than the strength of her propeller, and as the Captain stared at the ugly crack in the bright brass collar, his brain boiled with thoughts of the potentialities of tragedy.

The damage would have to be repaired before the vessel could venture to brave the Arctic seas. The only question was whether to put into Cape Town or try to make it on to Melbourne, the only two accessible points where a permanent repair could be made. Cape Town was the closest at hand, but Melbourne was on the preselected route, so Waddell boldly decided to make his way across the Indian Ocean under sail and put into the Australian port for the necessary repair work as soon as he could get there. It happened to be a very fortunate choice, considering that the Iroquois, unknown to the men of the Shenandoah, was in pursuit and close on the Shenandoah's trail.

The meridian of Greenwich was crossed on December 12 in a fresh west gale with a high running sea. The ship rolled very deeply on account of the large quantity of coal in her hold, and she also steered rather wildly owing to her being low by the head. But all sharp and narrow vessels of great length have a tendency to roll deeply, and great length has the virtue of giving stability in a wind.

Waddell had been instructed to cross the meridian of the Cape of Good Hope by the first of January, but he was well ahead of his schedule, and at noon on December 17 the Shenandoah was comfortably to the east of that meridian and bowling along with a west wind following fast.

As the hours passed, the wind steadily freshened, and soon it developed into a revolving gale of increasing violence, accompanied by squalls of snow and hail which made deck duty decidedly unpleasant and even dangerous. As the fury of the storm increased, the waves rose to fearsome heights, crashing down on the wallowing ship with a terrifying splatter, but the Shenandoah was a sturdy sailer, and she stood up under the furious buffeting of the gale in a way that made her officers proud of her.

Life aboard the cruiser during those trying days, however, was anything but comfortable. Sleep was almost out of the question, for the men could barely stay in their hammocks. It was next to impossible to get a meal in decent fashion. The steward, by the exercise of great ingenuity, might manage to get food cooked and transported triumphantly to the table, but the very next minute a heavy lurch of the ship would scatter dishes and contents in every direction and send the men sprawling out of their seats. Or a mountainous wave might come pouring over the rail, and, as the seams of the deck had sprung, the occupants of the cabins and forecastle never knew when they might be subjected to an involuntary shower.

Up on deck the batteries were secured with extra tackles, with the preventer braces and backstays rove and tautened. Hatches were battened down, and men were stationed at the relieving tackles, in case the wheel ropes should part, to prevent the ship from broaching to.

The cruiser drove before the gale at eleven knots under close-reefed topsails and reefed foresails; and the crew, in spite of the nasty weather, gathered in little groups at sheltered spots on the deck whenever opportunity offered and swapped yarns as they drank the extra grog which was issued during the storm. But there was little time available for even this limited relaxation. Nearly every hour brought some new danger, some fresh crisis, and the men must make their way, staggering as though drunk, across the slanting decks to their appointed places.

During the second day of the blow there came one supremely fearful moment when the struggling ship was near to foundering. A giant wave of extraordinary proportions came surging down amid cries of terror and discharged on the deck a cataract weighing hundreds of tons. Fore and aft the water stood on the deck level with the top of the bulwarks, and the ship, reeling under this unwonted load, lost headway and trembled in every rib with a harrowing shudder. There was pandemonium among the men as they splashed about in the water, struggling to regain their feet, but Lieutenant Grimball, the officer of the deck, kept as cool in the emergency as though such events were common in his young life. Instantly he perceived the imminence of the danger, and instantly acted to avert it. At his command members of the crew sprang forward with axes and with furious desperation dashed out the ports. The tremendous weight of water which was threatening to send the vessel to the bottom now spouted harmlessly back into the sea, and the ship, as though conscious of her deliverance from disaster, sprang forward eagerly before the driving wind.

After nerve-wracking days and nights of this the vessel ran out of the gale, for Captain Waddell had changed her course to the northward until she was above parallel 40°. Even after the wind had subsided, however, the seas continued to run high for three or four days, and the Shenandoah was knocked about like a cork in a mill race. But she managed to hold her course for Australia and steadily forged ahead.

But during those tempestuous days not all the stormy scenes originated without. Weeks of being cooped up together were beginning to fray the nerves of the men. The supersensitive captain was beginning to get an inkling of the fact that his officers did not have the fullest possible confidence in him. His feelings were still ruffled by the argument he had had with Whittle and Grimball and Lining the day they chased the British ship in the rain squall. There had been another argument as to whether they should put in at Tristan d'Acunha. Then, the last day in the Indian Ocean, while the storm raged, there was another unpleasant scene aboard, Chew being the central figure. Poor Chew was one of those bumbling individuals who seem born to misfortune, and recently he had been having a streak of it. One of the heavy seas shipped by the rolling Shenandoah had flooded his cabin and soaked all his possessions. In the next day of comparative calm, when he had taken his trunk on deck to dry its contents, a sudden vagrant gust of wind blew all his letters and most of his clothes overboard. The next day he lost his best new uniform cap while leaning over the rail. And meanwhile, all unknown to him, Captain Waddell was developing an acute distrust of Chew's seamanship. A squall was blowing up beneath the decks of the "Shenanigan," as the young officers had playfully dubbed the cruiser.

The explosion came on the night of December 16. It was blowing heavily, and big seas were running. About nine o'clock the captain called his first lieutenant.

"Mr. Whittle," he said, "Mr. Chew, I believe, has the mid-watch, and I am uneasy as to his capacity on a night like this. Will you be so good as to go below and tell him, if he is not asleep, that he will not be called for his watch but that Mr. Minor will be ordered to keep it?"

Chew, not unnaturally, was offended by this reflection on his ability, and after brooding over it all night sought out Lining the next morning to ask him what he ought to do about it.

"There is one thing certain," Lining assured him heartily, "and that is that your dignity and position as an officer will be injured unless you do something. You should go to the captain right now and protest. You'll sacrifice your self-respect if you don't."

Chew took his advice, but got no satisfaction from the stiff-necked commander. Waddell not only offered no apology or redress, but rubbed salt into Chew's wounded feelings by telling him flatly, "I should do it again should circumstances arise to make it advisable in my opinion."

Chew was not so far committed to his course that he could not retreat, and so asked to be relieved of duty, adding that at the first opportunity he would apply for permission to leave the ship. When he reported the outcome of his interview to Lining, the surgeon told him he had gone too far in suggesting that he would leave the vessel.

"You shouldn't be run off the ship like a whipped dog," he told him belligerently. "If I were in your place, the captain would have to be the one to send me off. I wouldn't leave voluntarily."

As the day wore on there was a growing feeling of tension aboard. Most of the officers sympathized with poor Chew. Maybe he wasn't the best seaman in the world, but to be relieved of his watch in time of stress and to be replaced by a petty officer was a double affront which could not go unnoticed. The captain could not be unaware of the fact that he had prodded a hornets' nest. As the mid-watch hour approached in the evening, the suspense grew. Would Chew be called for his watch? At length the kindly Whittle, presuming on his position as second in command, went to the captain and interceded with him.

"But I've no confidence in him in such weather," the captain sputtered.

Whittle, however, pressed the matter, and at length Waddell agreed to restore Chew to duty, under the equivocal conditions that "in very heavy seas" Whittle was to stand watch with him, to which Whittle agreed.

Waddell was thoroughly conscious of the officers' feelings in regard to his treatment of Chew, and it rankled.

"It seems that everybody has turned against me," he wailed querulously to Whittle.

When Whittle repeated this to Lining, the testy

doctor said sharply, "How childish that is! If he would only act like a real commander, we would all be with him."

So, amid storms without and storms within, the Shenandoah fought her way eastward toward Australia. The officers spent their spare time playing game after game of chess, and as Christmas approached, the holiday spirit mounted in them. On Christmas Eve Dr. Lining and the irrepressible Smith Lee sat up until midnight and then woke up all the officers for the drinking of a Christmas toast. "To our sweethearts and wives," the traditional Navy toast was downed, and then a round to "A return of many Christmases," and the revelers turned in to sleep late on Christmas morning. For some it was their first Christmas at sea. For even the oldest of the sailors it was about the roughest holiday they had ever spent.

"I have spent four Christmas days at sea," exclaimed Mr. Browne as he clung perilously to a swaying door-frame, "but this is the most miserable travesty of the festival I have ever celebrated."

Despite all the obstacles and all the ugly weather, however, an effort was made to celebrate the day in proper style. The cook had been jealously saving one of the geese obtained at Tristan d'Acunha for Christmas dinner. Old and tough though the bird was, the cook parboiled him and baked him to a crisp and sizzling brown. In addition to the goose, there were fresh pork, corned beef, potatoes, canned tomatoes, and mince pie. Despite the gyrations of the plunging vessel, the cook at last managed to deposit the holiday

meal on the wardroom table with a flourish of pride
and triumph. But before Captain Waddell could
say grace, an extraordinary lunge of the lurching
ship sent the goose and its platter skidding off onto
the deck, amid the loud lamentations of the officers.
But they refused to be deprived of the *pièce de ré-
sistance* of their Christmas dinner by any such Nep-
tunish prank, and the goose was quickly recovered
and restored to the place of honor on the table. "To
our absent ones" was the first toast proposed, and
the young officers, with their thoughts far away at
their homes in Virginia and Carolina and Mississippi, drained their glasses. But sad thoughts were
not to dampen the ardor of the laughing officers who
struggled with the tough old bird and wished each
other a Merry Christmas under the smoky lantern
that swung crazily from the wardroom ceiling.

On December 29, as the ship still wallowed in those
rolling seas under short canvas, a sail was reported
astern, and from the deck a ship could be dimly
discerned between the squalls of fine rain. As soon as
it could be ascertained what canvas she was carrying,
the Shenandoah was made to hold her luff to prevent
the stranger from passing out of gunshot to windward, and when she approached closely enough she
was brought to with a challenging gun.

It proved to be the American bark Delphine of
Bangor, bound for Akyab to load a cargo of rice intended for the provisioning of the Federal armies in
the field. Informed that his bark was a Confederate
prize and would be destroyed, Captain Nicholls
raised the issue that his wife and little boy were on

board, and also that the ship's steward was accompanied by his wife.

"Can't you permit us to continue on our way?" he pleaded. "It may cause the death of my wife to remove her. The report of your gun has made her ill!"

This introduced an unfamiliar and disturbing complication. Captain Waddell was the last man on earth to wish to cause the death of a noncombatant female, and Dr. Lining was called into consultation. The practical Dr. Lining, however, after quizzing the Yankee captain, advanced the opinion that if Mrs. Nicholls was suffering nothing more serious than shock from the noise of the gun it would certainly not endanger her life to remove her. Accordingly a bosun's chair was prepared, a whip fitted to the main yard, and soon the two women and the little boy were safely landed on the Shenandoah's decks. One of the crew gallantly carried Mrs. Nicholls' personal baggage, but she clutched tightly in her own hand a bright brass cage containing her pet canary, and the undismayed little bird chirped shrilly as they were set down on deck.

As the officer of the deck was conducting the women to the "ladies' cabin," they met Captain Waddell.

"Welcome on board the Shenandoah, ladies," said Waddell with his most courtly bow.

"Are you the captain?" Mrs. Nicholls demanded in stern tones.

The captain assured her that he was.

"Well, what are you going to do with us? Where will we be landed? I want to know."

Nettled by her manner, but always the gentleman,

Captain Waddell replied that if she so desired he would be glad to set her ashore on the nearest dry land, which happened to be the bleak and rocky island of St. Paul.

"Oh, no, never!" she protested in alarm. "I've seen that desolate place. I'd rather stay on your pirate ship than on that desert island." And the captain passed on without relieving her mind on that score.

Although courteous to the lady, Waddell did not mince any words when he encountered Captain Nicholls, a small, tired-looking man with a meek and apologetic manner.

"So that's your sick wife, is it?" he asked. "Why, she is as robust and healthy looking a woman as I ever saw. I am surprised at an honorable ship's captain resorting to such misrepresentations."

"Well, to tell you the truth," returned Nicholls weakly, "I am ashamed of myself. But she suggested it, Captain, and she has a way about her. And, anyhow, I didn't think it was a sin to tell a lie to try to save my ship.

"I've had a presentiment of trouble ever since we left London," he continued with the garrulity of a man whose conversational opportunities are rare. "Why, would you believe it, the very first day out my little boy, and he's just six years old, was spelling out the words in his Testament, and he pointed out to me the tenth verse of the twenty-seventh chapter of the Acts of the Apostles. I'll never forget it, sir: 'Paul admonished them and said unto them, Sirs, I perceive that the voyage will be with injury and much loss, not only of the lading and the ship, but also of our lives.' "

"Well," agreed Captain Waddell grimly, "you've lost the ship and the lading all right enough, but I believe I can assure you that your lives are in no danger. You needn't worry about that."

"I couldn't get it off my mind. It seemed to be surely an omen. Just think of that, captain—a little child, he's just six years old—" and poor Captain Nicholls babbled on and on.

But Captain Waddell tore himself away. "The gray mare is the better horse," he muttered to himself as he went about the task of superintending the burning of the Delphine. Mrs. Nicholls, as the flames ran lightly up the doomed ship's rigging, stood on the poop and made loud and bitter comments about the contemptibility of the pirates who burned her husband's ship and made prisoners of innocent women and children. Captain Nicholls himself, while his wife raged, suffered in silence, but he leaned abjectly on the rail and looked sorrowfully at his burning vessel until she sank below the horizon.

The mate of the Delphine assumed a surly and truculent attitude to his captors. When asked if they had any money aboard, he shrilled out, "Money? Money be damned! What the bloody hell do you think we'd be doing with money at sea? Don't talk like a damned fool." And when Lieutenant Grimball inquired if they had a supply of preserved meats or fruit on board, he laughed nastily. "Good God A'mighty, man! Are you hungry?" But at the threat

of irons he soon developed a less belligerent and more
co-operative frame of mind.

Captain Nicholls was chagrined when he had an
opportunity to examine the Shenandoah at close
range.

"Why this is just an imitation man-of-war," he exclaimed in mild disgust. "You fooled me all right. I
thought when I came aboard I'd find a real warship
with plenty of guns and plenty of men to work them
—a craft that would be ready to blow me out of the
water in five minutes' time. Why, if I'd known you
were like this, I'd have shown you my heels."

Captain Waddell himself was secretly inclined to
agree that had the Yankee shaken out his canvas, going at the rate he was, he could have given the cruiser
the slip before the shorthanded Shenandoah could
have made sail or brought her guns to bear. But he
made no such admission to his prisoner. His succession of successful captures was serving to build up
his confidence.

"You don't know us," he said darkly. "It's fortunate for you and your ladies you didn't make the
mistake of trying to run for it."

"Well, I'm not so sure of that," shrilly interposed
Mrs. Nicholls, coming up to join in the discussion. "I
told him all the time he ought to try to get away.
And now look what he's done! He's lost his ship—and
him with a third interest in her. And he's got me and
my little boy and my poor little bird here aboard this
pirate ship, and what will happen to us the Lord only
knows. Probably be set down on some God-forsaken
desert island to starve or to be devoured by cannibals,

and all because he wasn't spunky enough to try to get away. I told you—"

"Now, Lily, now, now—" soothed the poor captain and Waddell discreetly withdrew to the serene quiet of his cabin.

Having got out of the track of the storms, the Shenandoah now encountered a delightful spell of soft and balmy weather, and the first day of January, 1865, dawned a bright May-like day, with the sun shining and a light breeze blowing. At eight o'clock in the morning all hands were mustered on deck, and Captain Waddell impressively greeted the New Year by raising the Confederate ensign to the peak, selecting for the ceremony a new flag, fresh out of the locker, which had never before been unfurled to the winds of the sea.

The next day they sighted the forbidding shores of the desolate St. Paul islands in the Indian Ocean, a group made up of three tiny dots of rock, St. Paul, Amsterdam, and St. Denis, and the ship stood in for the purpose of regulating her chronometers and making observations. While this was being done, a party under Lieutenant Grimball was sent ashore on St. Paul's to investigate the possible presence of enemy shipping. The only signs of life, however, were provided by a party of ten Frenchmen who were on a periodic visit to the islands to catch and salt fish. Browne swapped his silk handkerchief to one of them for a hen and rooster, Dr. McNulty traded his waistcoat for a private supply of salt fish, and the hospitable Frenchmen gave them a supply of bait and showed them the best place in the harbor to fish. So when they returned to the cruiser in the evening they brought a boatload of fish which they had caught, a supply of eggs they had purchased, and Browne's newly acquired facilities for a future supply of eggs. In addition to these contributions to the ship's larder, they also brought back with them a penguin, and there was much merriment on board as this solemn looking bird stalked about the deck in all its ridiculous dignity. Some irrepressible soul pinned a rag around its neck resembling a shawl in its folds, and the sight of this broke down even the austerity of Mrs. Nicholls, who was beginning to show signs of making the best of her plight.

"Just like an old woman, for all the world!" she exclaimed, joining in the laughter of the men, and Captain Nicholls laughed too when he saw that she had unbent. Captain Nicholls was now in a more cheerful mood than he had been when the islands were first sighted. He had somehow gained the impression (probably from his wife) that it was Captain Waddell's intention to set him and his entourage ashore on St. Paul's, and as this out-of-the-way spot was seldom visited by vessels from the outside world, it might have meant remaining there in lonely solitude for years before a return to civilization could be effected. Mrs. Nicholls herself was firmly convinced of this also. She had taken Captain Waddell's casual ironic words at face value, and as they approached the islands tears started in her eyes at the prospect of being left there.

Seeing her tears, Hunt courteously inquired the

cause of her misgivings, and when she told him of her fears he hastened to reassure her.

"How could you ever imagine," he protested, "that Captain Waddell would think of leaving a whole ship's company, including ladies, in such a desolate place? That would be inhuman."

"Well," parried Mrs. Nicholls, "they tell terrible stories at home about the outrages committed upon defenseless men and women by your rebel cruisers. The papers have been full of them, and I naturally supposed they were true. You know, some of the papers say you are no better than pirates and that the only reason you don't fly the black flag is that for the time being it suits your convenience to sail under another that is not much more reputable."

Smiling at her outspoken avowal of her fears, Hunt asked to see some of the terrifying accounts to which she referred. She dug out of her baggage a number of copies of an illustrated New York publication in which was printed a blood-and-thunder narrative involving the activities of the Confederate cruiser Alabama, in which Admiral Semmes and his men were pictured as a lot of merciless cutthroats unfit to associate with such comparative paragons of marine virtue as Captain Kidd or Blackbeard. Hunt in great glee hurried off to the wardroom with this lurid narrative, and here for many days the young men enjoyed with much hilarity the reading and re-reading of this account of the misdeeds committed by the bloodthirsty ruffians sailing the sea under the Confederate flag.

The Shenandoah, despite her patched-up propeller, had of necessity been under steam while working in close to the islands, but she was now back in the open sea, ready to bank her fires and resume sailing. When the propeller was triced up, it was found that the band of the coupling was cracked again. Once more emergency repairs were resorted to, as well as could be done by the ship's mechanics, but the new break made it all the more imperative that Melbourne and its docking facilities be reached as soon as possible. Furthermore, Captain Waddell was anxious to reach that port in time to send off reports on a mail steamer which, Dr. Lining had told him, was scheduled to leave there January 26. Lining had told him the date of the mail steamer's sailing for the purpose of inducing him to delay his arrival in Melbourne until after her departure.

"She'll reveal our whereabouts to the world," he said. But Waddell did not care about that. So all sail was crowded on, and they flew along toward Australia as fast as a brisk wind would carry them.

The cruiser was now making smoother sailing, but among the officers and crew the storms continued. Quartermaster Hall, reporting for duty one morning with a pair of black eyes, explained that he had fallen down a ladder. Lieutenant Whittle cheerily asked him if he had hurt the ladder very much, then winking at the battered quartermaster, said sympathetically, "Hall, that fellow gave you particular hell, didn't he?"

"No, he didn't," protested Hall, quickly abandoning the flimsy story of his encounter with the ladder.

"In the first part of the fight he did punch me in the eyes and get a little the better of it, but after I got under weigh, sir, I made a monument of his nose."

And, sure enough, Dr. McNulty reported later that Sylvester had come to him for treatment of a badly battered nose and a pair of eyes even blacker than Hall's.

Such rumpuses among the crew and petty officers were not unexpected, but there were continuing evidences of the widening breach between the captain and his staff. Still impressed with Chew's lack of capacity, Waddell conceived the idea of relieving him of his watch entirely and appointing him a "prize master." The duties of the prize master, it developed, consisted in taking charge of all the captured sextants, chronometers, and navigation instruments and keeping the chronometers wound. Chew innocently accepted the quasi-promotion, and Minor took over his watch, but Dr. Lining, when Chew informed him of the transaction, sharply rebuked him for his gullibility.

"You have lowered yourself from an officer of the deck to a mere clock-winder," he sneered. "I am disappointed in you. Why, before I would consent to such a thing as that I would resign my commission."

But the placid Chew seemed satisfied and made no protest over his altered status. The change, however, was not taken so calmly in other quarters. Browne and Mason, the two midshipmen, ranked Minor, who was only a noncommissioned officer, and they protested to Whittle over his jumping them. They had both been disgruntled from the start of the cruise because of their being ranked below Bulloch, with whom they had formerly been on an equal footing. They had grudgingly acquiesced in being overslaughed, recognizing Bulloch's superior claims by reason of his experience on the Alabama. Minor, however, was a horse of another color, and they minced no words in making their complaint to the first lieutenant. Whittle presented their protest to the captain, but he was in no humor to entertain protests.

"It seems as though we're getting to a point where I'll have to ask my officers what I can do and what I can't do," he said to Whittle with heavy sarcasm—and that was the end of Browne's and Mason's protest. That is, it was the end so far as the captain was concerned. The two malcontent midshipmen brooded over it as the days went by.

Waddell, after sleeping over the matter, attempted to salve Chew's feelings by officially designating him ordnance officer. His announcement of this to Whittle precipitated another discussion of ship politics, during the course of which Whittle presumed to rebuke the captain for telling everybody where they were going. Waddell did not relish criticism, even from his chief officer, and an acrimonious dispute ensued.

"I'm very much afraid we are going to have trouble in this ship before this cruise is over," Dr. Lining said ominously to Smith Lee, and there seemed to be ample reason for his fears.

The matter was finally settled when Bulloch's eyes became so inflamed by taking the sights on the sun that he could not continue this duty, and another shake-up became necessary. Bulloch was put on

Chew's old watch, relieving Minor, and Chew was assigned to the sailing master's duty during Bulloch's incapacity for service. This removed any smirch on Chew's official dignity and also removed the cause for Mason's and Browne's disaffection, but it left everybody in a bad humor.

Friction of an unexpected but less serious nature threatened when Captain Nicholls began to manifest evidences of a latent streak of jealousy. Doctor Lining passed his thirty-first birthday on January 6, and the recurrence of his anniversary disturbed his emotional equilibrium and filled him with romantic thoughts about how he had spent his last birthday — seeing the sights of Florence while on a tour of Europe with a party which included "some sweet and pretty girls." In this mellow mood the young doctor even attempted to chat pleasantly with the formidable Mrs. Nicholls, and she thawed sufficiently under this unwonted attention to get out her album and show him her photographs. When Captain Nicholls came upon them thus engaged, he was furious and sternly called his spouse away from the tête-à-tête.

"The jealous old fool!" Lining exclaimed to Grimball, when the irate captain and his wife had departed to their cabin. "It's a fine state of affairs when a man thinks he has to watch his wife to keep her from doing wrong. I'm going to go on talking to her now all I can, just to plague him." And to show that he was in earnest he now began to play backgammon with Mrs. Nicholls at every opportunity in the evening, while the captain sat in his chair and fumed.

Captain Nicholls's display of jealousy was just

one evidence of the restoration of his drooping spirits. His chagrin at the loss of his vessel was being submerged in his growing interest in what was going on about him, and the longer he stayed on the cruiser, the more liberty he took in discussing the manner in which she was being handled. For one thing, he told Grimball, Waddell was too jittery and had himself called too frequently during the night.

"If I had a ship as large as this," he said, "and only five men in a watch, I'd like to see my mate call me before seven bells in the morning unless something very particular occurred. This Waddell is just an old woman."

Grimball gleefully repeated this criticism to Waddell, with the desired effect—the captain flew into a rage, denounced Nicholls as an ignorant old busybody, and expressed the hope that he might have an opportunity to "take some of the vanity out of him."

On the seventeenth there was a pleasant interlude. Early in the morning a sail was sighted—the Nimrod, an American-built ship, now sailing under the British flag. After investigation she was permitted to go on her way, and the captain, a giant with long whiskers, expressed his appreciation by coming off in his gig and bringing to Captain Waddell a present of a dozen bottles of fine old wine. By way of partially explaining his generosity he mentioned that he had married a New Orleans woman.

The previous day had been Lieutenant Whittle's twenty-fifth birthday, and there was a slightly belated celebration of the event with the assistance of the gift of wine. That night there was unwonted revelry and gaiety in the Shenandoah's wardroom, and the name of the Nimrod, although a neutral and not a captive, was long remembered pleasantly by the cruiser's officers.

No more vessels were encountered during the following week, and on the morning of the twenty-fifth the mainland of Australia was sighted at Cape Otway. Soon the Heads of Port Philip came into view, and here they were boarded by the health officers and a pilot, Mr. Johnson—all very much astonished to discover the identity and character of the visitor.

A little after sunset the pilot set her down in Hobson's Bay, where she dropped her anchors, and as the news of her arrival had been telegraphed from the Heads by the health officers there, she was given a tumultuous welcome which warmed and thrilled the adventurous little crew so far away from friends and home. Hardly had she dropped her anchors before a veritable fleet of small boats was swarming about her sides, with shouts of friendly greeting and congratulation. Captain Waddell, however, gave strict orders that no one be permitted to board her, as it was still problematical what attitude would be assumed by the Australian authorities.

But there was one earnest individual who would not be denied—an old man in a little sailboat rocking alongside the big ship, whose anxiety to set foot on her decks was pathetic and at the same time ludicrous. Repeatedly denied in his entreaties, he at length climbed the spar of his little boat and, watching his opportunity, sprang nimbly into the cruiser's mizzen chains and scrambled triumphantly onto the deck.

There was something so laughably audacious in being thus so summarily boarded, in defiance of orders, by a solitary but persistent individual that Chew, the officer of the deck, was at a loss what course to pursue, whether to throw him overboard or reward his audacity by surrendering the ship to him.

But the unmistakably friendly light in the ingenious visitor's eye defied an angry reception.

"I just had to set foot on you," he expostulated. "I'm the only genuine Confederate in all Australia. Don't that entitle me to a reception on board any vessel that flies my country's flag?"

"Well, I don't know about that," mused Chew, "I'm not very well up on international law. But, at any rate, you're here now, if it does you any good, and if you'll keep out of the skipper's sight, I'll not have the boys throw you over the rail—which is what I probably ought to do."

Delighted with even this limited manifestation of Southern hospitality, the old man stood fondly gazing at the flag at her peak. And thus the roving cruiser was received in Australia by the nearest thing to a Confederate ambassador.

Immediately upon dropping anchor, Captain Waddell, always a stickler for the official niceties and proprieties, sent Lieutenant Grimball ashore with an official communication, addressed to His Excellency Sir Charles H. Darling, K. C. B., Captain General and Governor in Chief and Vice-Admiral:

"I have the honor to announce to your excellency the arrival of the C. S. S. Shenandoah, under my command, in Port Philip this afternoon, and also to communicate that the steamer's machinery requires repairs and that I am in need of coal. I desire your excellency to grant permission that I may get the necessary repairs and supply of coal to enable me to get to sea as quickly as possible. I desire also your excellency's permission to land my prisoners."

Mr. Grimball returned at ten o'clock that evening with word that an official reply would be forthcoming the following day. He found Waddell just blotting the ink of the last words of his official communication to Secretary Mallory to be mailed next day in care of Bulloch in London.

The problem of the prisoners, however, solved itself, as the prisoners did not await official permission to land. Early the next morning Captain Waddell was awakened by the noise of voices in the adjoining cabins, from which it was clear that they were preparing to take French leave. Furthermore, it was obvious from her words that Mrs. Nicholls did not intend to depart empty handed.

"If you had any spunk," she was telling her spouse, "you'd make him give you back your chronometer and sextant. Why don't you stand up for yourself? I'm going to claim as my personal property all the books he took off the Delphine and save them for you. He won't refuse to give them to a lady."

True to her word, she claimed ownership of the books, and they were all turned over to her without protest—that is, all but one. Mr. Whittle, going through the books for possible new reading matter when they were first brought aboard the cruiser, had come across a copy of *Uncle Tom's Cabin* and in high bad temper had thrown it overboard.

"If it hadn't been for that lying book," he exclaimed, "we'd all be at home, comfortably enjoying ourselves right now."

Captain Waddell was careful to explain to the Delphine's prisoners that he had no authority to permit them to leave the vessel and that they could not use the Shenandoah's boats for that purpose. But they were determined to go, and he was so glad to be rid of them that he offered no obstacle when they called a shore boat to take them off. Into it they piled all their baggage, and the last the Shenandoah's men saw of Mrs. Nicholls, she was seated in the small boat's stern, her bird-cage in her lap, turning back to shake her fist at the cruiser as she cried out in her shrill voice, "I hope that dirty pirate may be burned!"

CHAPTER TEN

AN UNWELCOME GUEST
"DOWN UNDER"

IN CAPTAIN WADDELL'S LOG the entire stay in Australia is covered by this brief entry: "January 26–February 17. Repairing in Hobson's Bay, Australia." But back of that terse and colorless epitome, there is a long and complicated story of political intrigue, personal difficulties, threatened hostilities, wrangling, charges and countercharges, and international complications the repercussions of which were not finally quieted until the meeting of the tribunal at Geneva in 1868.

The arrival of the cruiser created a small furor in Melbourne, and the next morning after she dropped her anchors in the harbor the *Daily Herald* carried a prominently displayed account of it. "The men," said the *Herald* reporter, "are a fine and determined looking set of fellows. The uniform worn is a sort of yellowish gray, with a shoulder-strap of blue silk bearing a single star, surrounded by a thin gold cording. The cap is also gray, with a broad gold band." In the course of the article it was also men-

123

tioned that the Shenandoah was recognized in Melbourne shipping circles as "the Clyde-built Sea King, which made one of the fastest trips on record when she brought troops to Auckland last year."

Blanchard, the United States consul in Melbourne, that day sat down and wrote to Adams in London notifying him of the enemy cruiser's arrival. "It is not unlikely that she will next turn up in the Pacific," he wrote, "if she can hold together long enough. The officers on board declare that it would not be safe to fire a broadside, and it is the general impression that she is not a formidable vessel. She is leaking, and it takes two hours to pump her out."

"You've got a lot of friends in Melbourne," Pilot Johnson had told Captain Waddell when he boarded the ship at the Heads. This was true, too, but it was also true that they had active enemies there as well in the person of the consul and his satellites. And also they had the problem of neutrality, complicated by the governor's fear that he might commit some infraction of his instructions from London. The governor himself seemed friendly enough, although he was careful not to compromise his official neutrality. A majority of his council, however, were frankly inimical to the Southern cause. This was notably true of James G. Francis, the Commissioner of Trade and Customs, who was part owner of a shop which dealt in American goods and notions and who was a close political and business friend of Blanchard.

Captain Waddell immediately upon his arrival had requested an appointment for an official conference with Governor Darling, and Sir Charles set

12:30 the next day as the time for the audience. Captain Waddell was there on the minute, accompanied by an escort consisting of Grimball, Scales, and Lining—all dressed in their best uniforms and wearing their dress swords. To the meticulous Waddell's indignant surprise, the Governor was not in his office when they arrived, so the little party of Confederates left their cards and their regrets and stiffly departed.

"Aren't you going to wait a few minutes for him?" Mr. Grimball asked, but the unbending captain snorted an indignant negative.

"We represent the government of the Confederate States of America," he pointed out crisply. "It would not become us to kick our heels in his waiting room."

Hardly had they entered their conveyance and driven off before they passed the Governor in his carriage on his way to his offices. The practical Grimball suggested that they turn back and keep the appointment belatedly, but Waddell's conception of the dignity of their position was too lofty to admit of any such compromise.

"No," he said, positively and finally. "An hour was appointed. The Governor was not there. Let him take the next step."

So the party returned to Scott's, one of the leading hotels of Melbourne, where they laid aside their swords and had lunch, and then embarked on an afternoon of sightseeing in the strange Antipodean city. Back at Scott's for dinner, the visiting Confederate officers found themselves lionized and overwhelmed with preprandial hospitality. It was hard to refuse a glass with a friendly stranger who proposed "To the Southern Confederacy" or "To Jefferson Davis." So toast after toast was drunk, until the floor of Scott's barroom rocked like the bosom of the stormy Indian Ocean through which they had so recently passed. But the captain and Lieutenant Grimball eventually made it safely back to their cabins on the cruiser, while Scales and Lining spent the evening at the home of a local Confederate sympathizer, Mr. Knage, who hastily invited in his neighbors to meet his distinguished guests.

Governor Darling, despite his tardiness at his appointment, was conscious of the official attention due the visiting man-of-war, and the next morning Captain Waddell received a letter from Mr. Francis:

"I have received the instructions of Sir C. Darling to state that he is willing to allow the necessary repairs to the Shenandoah and the coaling of the vessel at once proceeded with, and that the necessary directions have been given accordingly." It was, however, requested "that you will be good enough, at your earliest convenience, to intimate to me, for the information of his excellency, the nature and extent of your requirements as regards repairs and supplies in order that Sir C. Darling may be enabled to judge of the time which it may be necessary for the vessel under your command to remain in this port."

Captain Waddell replied that his immediate needs consisted of fresh meat, vegetables, and bread daily, and that the sea supplies needed were brandy, rum, champagne, port, sherry, beer, porter, molasses, lime juice, and light material for summer clothing. As to the repairs necessary, he enclosed a letter from Lang-lands Brothers & Company, proprietors of the Port Philip Foundry, stating that their inspection, by a diver, revealed that, aside from the damage to the propeller, the lining of the outer stern-post was entirely gone. This, he reported, made it absolutely necessary to put the Shenandoah on "the government slip," and the repairs would require ten days.

Sir Charles, to make his position secure, appointed a committee consisting of Payne, inspector and secretary of the steam navigation board, Elder, superintendent of the marine yard, and Wilson, the government marine engineer, to go on board the Shenandoah to make an examination and report to him whether the vessel was actually in a fit state to proceed to sea, or what repairs were necessary. Captain Waddell consented to this official examination, and urged His Excellency that assistance be given him in hurrying up the work of repair as much as possible "as I am extremely anxious to get the Shenandoah to sea."

On February 1 the committee reported that it was evidently necessary for the ship to go into the slip, termed "the government patent slip," although, as Mr. Francis was careful to point out, it had long since passed out of the government's possession into private hands and arrangements for docking would have to be made with the private lessees.

Accordingly the ship was prepared to be placed in the slip, but immediately difficulties ensued. The executive council decreed that the government shears could not be used for lifting the Shenandoah's screw, as that might be construed as a violation of strict neutrality. While this red tape was being untangled, Francis wrote to Captain Waddell pointing out that the Shenandoah had already been in port for twelve days and stating that "it is now desired by His Excellency that you should now name the day upon which you will be prepared to proceed to sea."

Waddell, nettled by the tone of this letter, replied that he could hardly be expected to name the day of his departure when he had not yet been able to get his ship into the slip where the injury could be seen and an estimate made of the time needed for the repairs. Heavy weather had prevented the lightening of the ship necessary to bring her draft down sufficiently to get into the dock, but he hoped to have this done by February 8. On February 14 Mr. Francis again asked that a date of departure be set, and Mr. Waddell informed him that Langland Brothers & Company expected to have the Shenandoah ready for launching the next day and that, without unforseen accident, she should be able to proceed to sea by Sunday the nineteenth.

While the ship was still lying at anchor, anonymous warnings had been received of an alleged plot by American sympathizers to destroy her by means of a torpedo. Extra watches were established on board the vessel, and nobody was permitted to come near her at night. The police superintendent, Thomas Lyttleton, was also notified, and he issued instructions to the water police to keep a close watch on the visitor, and although no signs of any plot of destruction developed, the nerves of all on board were taut.

Then there were other complications. Seven members of the crew of the Shenandoah, all of them recruits from the captured vessels, had gone ashore and deserted. Waddell quickly notified Richard C. Standish, chief commissioner of police, requesting that the police give assistance to the ship's officers in arresting the deserters and returning them to the ship. Standish coldly replied that the law did not require him to render such assistance. Whereupon nine more of the recruits deserted, and Captain Waddell raged helplessly at the supineness of the police.

The strained relations were almost brought to the breaking point on February 13, when Captain Lyttleton came on board the Shenandoah, armed with a search warrant, and announced that he had been instructed to search the ship for a man described only as "Charlie" who was alleged to have joined the crew since the vessel arrived in the harbor, in defiance of the neutrality laws. Waddell assured him that no additional members had been signed to the crew since the vessel arrived, but Lyttleton was unconvinced.

"I've got straight information from former members of your crew, Captain," he insisted, "and I can bring them here and let you hear them. One thing I must insist on, however. If I introduce these witnesses on the deck of your vessel for the purpose of identifying the man, if he is found on board, will they be given protection, even though they may be deserters from your ship?"

This touched Captain Waddell on the tender spot of his official dignity and rights as a commander.

"The deck of the Shenandoah represents Confederate territory," he replied sternly. "Every violation of the law or the usage of the sea service committed on her deck will be punished by the laws which govern the ship. These 'witnesses' you mention are classified on our list as deserters, and if any deserter from the Shenandoah appears on her deck, it matters not under what circumstances, he shall most certainly be arrested.

"Furthermore, Captain Lyttleton, let me state just as emphatically as I can make it that your application to search the vessel is refused, and should the Victoria government attempt so great an outrage, the Shenandoah will be defended at every risk to life. I bid you a good afternoon, Captain."

Before dismissing Lyttleton, however, Captain Waddell made a gesture of co-operation by ordering a thorough search of the ship by Grimball and the master-at-arms to see if "Charlie" could be found. They reported "no strangers on board," and the skeptical Lyttleton was forced to depart with this equivocal verdict. After he had gone, Bulloch, with a belated display of conscience, confided in Dr. Lining that he knew of some stowaways on board. At Lining's prompting he revealed this knowledge to Whittle, and the stowaways were promptly hunted out and set ashore. The Melbourne papers the next morning stated that one of the ejected men was none other than the mysterious and elusive "Charlie," and that he had been arrested and held for trial on the charge of violating the foreign enlistment act. But by the time this information reached Waddell the question had become a purely academic one, and meanwhile he had successfully maintained the integrity of his

legal status and the dignity of the Southern Confederacy.

Francis bubbled with indignation upon being informed of Captain Waddell's position, and wrote him
a sharp letter in which he said that "you are ap-
pealed to to reconsider your determination; and
pending a further intimation from you, which you
are requested to make with as little delay as possible,
the permission granted you to repair and take supplies is suspended."

But Captain Waddell had been sitting up nights
reading his Phillemore and his Wheaton. He knew his
rights and had made up his mind. To buttress his
position, however, he called a council of his officers,
and for once they all agreed with him and col-
laborated in his reply.

"According to all the laws of nations," he wrote,
"the deck of a vessel of war is considered to represent
the majesty of the country whose flag she flies." And
he ended his letter by saying: "And I, in the name of
the government of the Confederate States of America, hereby enter my solemn protest against any ob-
struction which may cause the detention of this ship
in this port."

Enraged at this defiance of Her Brittanic Majesty, Francis hastily telegraphed to Beaver of the
water police at Williamstown instructing him to sur-
round the slip with his whole force of police and to
prevent the launching of the ship "at all risks." All
the militia of Melbourne were turned out under arms.
The artillery companies were sent to the beach, where
they unlimbered and trained their guns on the Con-

federate vessel, and the lessee of the slip was instructed to desist at once from rendering any aid or
assistance or performing any work on the Shenandoah or in launching the vessel. Having committed
these overt acts, Francis cooled off enough to seek
legal advice as to whether he, as an agent of the government, was acting within his rights, and he was
promptly informed by the Queen's counsel that "the
government have not the power which they claim"
and that the action taken with respect to the Shenandoah constituted "an unauthorized detention."

The next morning, therefore, Francis, inwardly
seething at being forced to back down, wrote to Captain Waddell explaining lamely that "the lessee of
the patent slip having reported that the safety of the
ship Shenandoah may be endangered by her present
position on the slip, the suspension of permission to
British subjects to assist in launching the ship is
withdrawn." And he was careful to add: "It is expected that you will exercise every dispatch so as to
insure your departure by the day named in your first
letter of yesterday, viz., Sunday next."

While all this interchange of correspondence with
a hostile official was keeping Captain Waddell in a
feverish stew of worry and apprehension, the other
officers of the Shenandoah were having the time of
their lives. Regardless of the governor's careful neutrality, regardless of the studied hostility of Francis,
a goodly proportion of the people of Melbourne and
the surrounding country were openly sympathetic

with the Confederate cause and they lionized the young Southern officers.

The second day after the ship's arrival in port she was thrown open to the inspection of visitors. Steamers and sailboats immediately came flocking off toward the cruiser at her anchorage, and until far into the evening were plying between ship and shore, bringing on board and taking away thousands of persons, some attracted by admiration and some by sheer curiosity. The public's interest in the visiting cruiser was astonishing, and on the first Sunday after her arrival she was visited by more than 8,000 people.

The officers displayed their best grade of Southern hospitality, but privately they expressed their regret that there were so few pretty girls among the visitors, and they were sometimes secretly amused by the questions asked. A large percentage of the Australians, it seemed, had swallowed without question the theory that all Confederate cruisers were pirates, and they took it for granted that when a Yankee prize was scuttled or burned the men on board were left to their fate. But even those who entertained such beliefs in the bloodthirsty character of the Rebels nevertheless took pride in going through the vessel so that they might afterwards boast that they had visited on board the pirate craft.

There were many other visits from petty government understrappers, who were not at all backward in asking pointed and impertinent questions about the cruiser and its future activities.

"Where will you go from here?" one of the snoopers ingenuously asked Whittle, who was in charge in the Captain's absence.

"Do you suppose I would be such a damned fool as to tell you if I knew?" he replied pleasantly.

As the people swarmed on board, not a few of them felt out the officers about the possibility of enlisting for the remainder of the cruise. But the officers were deeply suspicious of all who made such advances and repelled them very firmly. No less than forty-seven letters were received during the cruiser's stay applying for service in the Shenandoah, to none of which was reply made, the Captain suspecting all of them of being bogus, sent to trap him into a violation of neutrality.

He was particularly suspicious of an old lady who came on board the ship several times, accompanied by a little boy twelve years old who she said was her grandson. She was too infirm to support the lad any longer, she said, and since they had both been born in Mobile, she asked that the boy be permitted to ship on board in the Confederate service. She was directed to apply to the attorney-general in Melbourne for advice in her case, and instructed not to renew her application unless supplied with a certificate setting forth her indisputable right to enter the lad in the Confederate service. She never came back, which confirmed Captain Waddell's suspicions.

"I knew she was a fraud the minute I laid my eyes on her," he said.

But most of the visitors were free from guile. They came to see and to admire. The ladies beamed on the officers and fluttered with pleasure when they could

134

get one of them to show them over the boat. Life on board the ship was one continuous levee during those visitors' days, really almost as strenuous as cruising, and after two or three days of this, it was found necessary to hang out the "No Visitors" sign. The populace's interest in the Confederates and admiration for them continued, however, and whenever officers or men went ashore they were overwhelmed with attentions.

"Had we accepted a tenth of the invitations we received to indulge in spirituous comforts," one of them wrote later, "we should all of us, from the Captain down to the toughest old shellback in the forecastle, have been shockingly inebriated for the whole period of our sojourn."

As a matter of fact, there was some drunkenness. One evening a jovial party was in progress at Scott's, where there were fifteen or twenty gathered around the table, including a few of the Shenandoah's officers, eating dinner and indulging in an occasional patriotic toast. While the festivities were at their peak, and after a number of toasts had been drunk, an uninvited guest entered the room, and, upon seeing the gray uniforms of the officers, launched into a tirade against the Southern Confederacy and all the rebel pirates in its service. When he began to draw a bit too freely upon his vocabulary of profane invective, Surgeon McNulty sprang to his feet and with one well aimed blow to the point of the intruder's chin sent him sprawling on the floor. In an instant a general brawl was in progress. Glasses and decanters flew through the air. Knives flashed. There were even pistol shots, but there was no bloodshed. The Shenandoah men emerged from the affray with their honor untarnished, though their uniforms were in a state of slight disarray. Then, after the Yankee sympathizer and his supporters had fled, the exuberant officers marched off in a body to the theatre, singing "The Bonnie Blue Flag."

Not all of the social affairs, however, were of so disorderly and boisterous a nature. Soon after the arrival of the cruiser the officers were entertained by the Melbourne Club at a formal dinner characterized by the greatest sobriety, decorum, and dignity. Some sixty guests, including the social leaders of Melbourne, sat down at the dinner, the president of the club at the head of the table with Captain Waddell on his right and the always-popular Smith Lee on his left. There was some apprehension among the guests about the toasts, but their tactful hosts permitted no embarrassment to arise. Only two toasts were drunk. First, of course, was the old British stand-by, "The Queen," which all drank standing. Then the Australians all rose to their feet again as the president of the club proposed "To the captain and officers of the Shenandoah, our guests of the evening," which was followed by three lusty cheers—a manifestation of enthusiasm which was unprecedented in the annals of the club and indeed prohibited by its rules.

None of the parties accorded them was more welcome than that given by Brayton, formerly of New York but then a gold mining speculator at Ballarat, forty miles away. Brayton's invitation came on the evening of the attempted seizure of the cruiser in the slip, and was therefore all the more welcome as affording a relief from the tension of that unpleasant day. All of the officers of the ship had been given passes on the railroad immediately upon their arrival, and they all took train for Ballarat in the afternoon of the fourteenth. They were met at the station by a crowd estimated at 2,000, accompanied by a brass band, and their progress to the scene of the party was a procession of triumph. One of the young men afterward wrote of the event:

"It was a decidedly *recherché* affair. The wealth, beauty, and fashion of Ballarat were out in full force, fully intent upon lionizing and doing honor to a few of the unpretending supporters of a young government battling for existence with the lusty giant of the Western world. Every attention that kindness and courtesy could suggest was shown us, and more than one heart beat quicker at such convincing evidence of the existence of sympathy in this country of the Antipodes for the service in which we were engaged. Many a gray uniform coat lost its gilt buttons that night, but we saw them again ere we bade a final adieu to Australia, suspended from watch-guards depending from the necks of bright-eyed women, and we appreciated the compliment thus paid, not to us but to our country. God bless the gentle women of Melbourne and Ballarat."

But at last all the balls and the dances and the wining and dining had to end. On the afternoon of February 15 the Shenandoah left the slip, cheered by a crowd of spectators gathered on the adjacent

wharves and saluted by the colonial steamer of war
Victoria. She was immediately taken alongside a col-
lier, the John Fraser, which had recently arrived
from Cardiff loaded with steamer coal, and there
loaded with 250 additional tons of fuel. The John
Fraser bore a name which sounded suspiciously Confederate, and her providential arrival in Melbourne
just in time to supply the cruiser with coal excited
some suspicion. It was suggested that the shrewd
Bulloch had despatched the John Fraser with its all-
important cargo from Cardiff at the time the decision
was made to send the Shenandoah on its cruise, but
all the officers on the cruiser protested ignorance of
any such arrangement. It was just a happy coinci-
dence, they assured everyone.

The coaling completed, preparations were made to
get away on the eighteenth, but there was one more
flurry of excitement. One of the unwilling members of
the Shenandoah's crew who had deserted when the
ship reached Melbourne was Andrew Forbes, and
Blanchard, the American consul, had hired him to
snoop around the waterfront during the cruiser's
stay and report any suspicious happenings. Late in
the afternoon of the seventeenth Forbes arrived
breathless at Blanchard's home, explaining between
gasps that he had run all the way from Sandridge.

"Is there anything suspicious afoot?" inquired
Blanchard eagerly.

"Suspicious?" repeated Forbes, "It's more than
suspicious. They're fixing to do it right now!"

"Do it? Do what? Who is going to do it?"

"I was down on the railway pier this afternoon,"

Forbes began, "down at Sandridge, you know, when I saw these five chaps standing there, all dressed better than usual, four chaps I had met down there at the Mariners' Home in Williamstown. You know you told me to mix around and get to know all the seafaring men."

"Yes, yes," interrupted Blanchard, "get on with your story. Who were they and what about them?"

"Well, they was Tom Evans and Bob Dunning and Charley Bird and Bill Green and little Sam—I don't know his last name—"

"Never mind his last name," put in Blanchard. "What were they doing there?"

"That's just what I asked them. I went up and spoke to them and I said to Tom, I said: 'What are you chaps doing down here?' But Tom, it seemed like, didn't want to tell me, and I said to him, I said: 'Well, Tom, you know you can trust me if it's a secret. What's up?' We talked back and forth and finally Tom said 'Oh, I suppose I needn't be scared to tell you, but keep your lip buttoned up. We're waiting here for the boats from the Maria Ross. That's her out there in the bay, ready for sea, and the boats will be here for us at five o'clock, and there's a lot more besides us going on her.' So I said—"

"Well, what about it? I'm not interested in the Maria Ross. It's the Shenandoah I'm interested in. If they weren't going aboard the Shenandoah, I don't care where they're going."

"Yes, sir. I'm coming to that. It seems as how the Maria Ross is going to meet the Shenandoah when she gets outside the Heads, and all these men that are going out aboard the Maria Ross will be taken aboard the Shenandoah from small boats through the propeller hoist-hole. Tom said there was forty or fifty of 'em going out on the Maria Ross, and—"

"Well, why didn't you say so," exploded Blanchard. "What have you been beating around the bush for? Come on, get your hat. We must hurry around to see Mr. Gurner, the crown solicitor, and put a stop to this."

With the still panting Forbes at his heels, Blanchard hurried toward Gurner's office to lodge an official complaint. They met Gurner, a beefy, florid man, at the gate in the very act of departure.

"Sorry, very sorry," he rumbled, tapping on the pavement impatiently with his ebony walking cane, "but I'm off to dinner and can't be detained. See me tomorrow." And he started off.

"But, sir," protested the consul, "I come as a representative of the United States government, with evidence to lay before you, the Crown Solicitor, of a large number of men about to violate your neutrality laws. Something must be done about it at once. Tomorrow will be too late."

But Mr. Gurner was not a man to let a little thing like international affairs interfere with him when his dinner was waiting.

"I don't care about all that. I want my dinner, and I'm going to have it. You've almost made me late now, keeping me standing here with all your talking. There are plenty of magistrates around town—go to some of them." As he stepped into his carriage, he shouted back, "My dinner! Lord, that's what I want!"

Astonished but undismayed by the behavior of the gourmet solicitor, Blanchard then hastened resolutely to Standish's office, but Standish was not in. Then off they rushed to the houses of parliament to consult the attorney general. This official listened patiently and respectfully to the consul's story, but said that he could not act without affidavits.

"I do not at all mean to discredit your relation of the facts," he explained courteously, "but I must be fortified with affidavits before I can take any official action."

Affidavits would take too long. Blanchard, now frantic with frustration, turned in desperation to the office of the detective police, where he excitedly poured out his story to Nicholson, the chief. Nicholson heard him through with true British calm and urbanity, but then reminded him that he could make no arrests without a warrant.

"Have you a warrant?"

No, Blanchard had no warrant, so off he raced to the police magistrate, Sturt, to get that necessary document.

Sturt also was polite and apparently sympathetic.

"But," he pointed out, "I can not take the responsibility of issuing a warrant on one man's testimony in such a grave affair. I should advise your going to see Mr. Call at Williamstown. He may have some evidence from the water police."

But Forbes was decidedly shy about returning to

Williamstown. The Confederate sympathizers there knew him for what he was, a turncoat and a spy, and Forbes flatly refused to risk his skin by venturing among them again.

Poor Blanchard, balked at every turn, was at his wits' end, but he still did not give up. Acting in his own official capacity, he hastily made a deposition himself, setting forth that a violation of the neutrality laws was about to be committed or was even then in progress, and this deposition he sent off to the attorney general. But in a few minutes the messenger returned reporting that the attorney general's office was closed for the night.

It was now nine o'clock. The faithful and conscientious Blanchard had exhausted every possible line of action and had accomplished nothing. His zeal and energy were powerless against the impregnable strength of official red tape. Baffled, he reluctantly and sadly went home and went to bed.

While Blanchard was rushing vainly about Melbourne, the Shenandoah was riding at single anchor, under steam, and ready for sea. The captain in his cabin was supplying a representative of the Melbourne *Argus* with a complete copy of his correspondence with the Australian officials. The reporters wanted it for its news value, and Captain Waddell was glad to have it published in the paper as a means of conveying it to Commodore Barron in Paris and through him to Secretary Mallory in Richmond.

The newspaper men disposed of, Waddell prepared to turn in for the night. Ready to get to sea again, he was well pleased with the outcome of his stay in Melbourne. As he relaxed in his berth he thought over the tumultuous events of the past few days, and his self-confidence waxed strong within him. Obstacle after obstacle had confronted him, and he had surmounted them all.

True, there had been some further evidences of friction among the personnel. The very first day in port he had had words with Dr. Lining because Dr. McNulty had been given permission to go ashore without consultation with Lining, McNulty's superior. Lining had not hesitated to voice his dissatisfaction with such an "informal style" of command, and predicted that it would lead to trouble. This prediction had been abundantly supported by events when McNulty, during their stay in port, developed an increasingly surly manner and became distressingly irregular in his habits. Indeed the final arrangements for sailing had to be held up while Midshipmen Mason and Browne were sent ashore to find the errant assistant surgeon and bring him aboard.

Then there had been trouble with Guy, the gunner's mate. Refused permission to go ashore one evening, he had stolen a boat and gone off without leave. When he returned he was met at the side ladder by Bulloch, who refused to allow him on board.

"You have no place on this ship now," Bulloch told him with cold severity. "You are marked on the roll as a deserter." Guy refused to accept this verdict and pushed his way up the ladder, but the resolute Bulloch tore Guy's shoulder straps from his jacket and kicked him down the steps into the boat.

But all this was past history now. Guy had been pardoned and restored to duty. McNulty was sobering up in his bunk. Lining, if dissatisfied, was quiescent. The Captain was feeling serene and confident.

At seven o'clock on the morning of February 18 the Shenandoah's anchors were on her bows, and away she steamed from the anchorage toward the Heads of Port Philip, with Pilot Johnson again at the wheel.

Poor Johnson had had bad luck since the day he brought the Senandoah into port, three weeks before. Bringing another vessel up the channel he had run her on a shoal, and since this mishap he had had difficulty in getting assignments. In his distress he had a friend speak to Captain Waddell in his behalf.

"Captain," he said, "if you will let Johnson take the Shenandoah to sea on her outward trip it will put him back on his feet. Give him some favorable publicity, you know."

So the generous Waddell engaged him on the spot, and Johnson took the cruiser outside the Heads with all his oldtime éclat.

The outward passage was not without its anxieties. There had been rumors in Melbourne that Yankee warships lurked outside, and bets had been offered that the Shenandoah would not pass through the Heads in safety. These rumors were discounted aboard the cruiser, but Waddell was taking no chances. Accordingly all her guns had been loaded, and the gun crews were mustered to their stations as she lifted her anchors. But the passage down the bay and outside was unmarked by any sign of trouble, and after dropping the pilot she stood away to the open sea.

Melbourne buzzed with rumors after the Shenandoah had cleared. One of the more fantastic of them was that Admiral Semmes had secretly boarded her before she left and was now in command. Some said she had shipped not less than a hundred new recruits while in port. Others said that her machinery was little more than patched up and that she probably wouldn't stay afloat more than thirty days.

The Daily *Argus* in an editorial said, "With all the sympathy we may have had with her as the representative of those who are gallantly fighting against long odds, she, in the fulfilment of a warlike errand, was most unwelcome in our still peaceful port, and we are unfeignedly glad of her departure."

The cruiser's bunkers were chock-full of the precious coal that might be so sorely needed in the long cruise ahead of her, and piled on the spar deck was an extra supply of coal in bags to be used in steaming out to the western edge of the South Pacific. She continued under steam until Cape Howe bore N.N.W. by compass, but then sail was made and the propeller triced up again.

At this juncture, there appeared on deck a motley lot of strangers, forty-five of them, who had concealed themselves about the vessel before she left the bay and now came out of their places of hiding. Twenty had hidden in some unused water tanks. Fourteen had crept into the hollow iron bowsprit, where they almost smothered, and another bunch of them were in the lower hold. But at last the whole lot of them were mustered forward, and word was passed to the captain to learn his pleasure.

When the captain appeared, he professed to be very much surprised and very much out of humor with the culprits.

"What are you fellows doing aboard this ship? What is your nationality, and what is your purpose here?"

They knew the answer to that one. Cockney and Spaniard and Yankee alike, they all answered gravely that they were natives of the Southern Confederacy and that they had secretly come aboard, of their own volition, for the purpose of enlisting under her banner. The officer of the deck for the preceding night could not account for their presence. He had kept a strict watch, he said, fearful that some unscrupulous persons might attempt to come on board in Australian waters in violation of the neutrality laws. Not a man Jack, he stoutly maintained, had come over the rail the night before.

Captain Waddell frowned and shook his head at the laxity which had permitted all these men to come aboard unknown to him.

"But," said he resignedly to Whittle, "here they are. I can swear that I personally had nothing to do with their coming aboard. I shall not insult you by asking if you knew anything about it beforehand. It develops, by their own statement, that they are citizens of the South. Is there any reason why they should not be mustered in as members of the crew?"

Whittle could think of no such reason, so forty-five

enthusiastic Confederates, most of whom could speak English plainly, were added to the ship's list, bringing the crew up to seventy-two men, equal to any emergency. In fact, Whittle now had available a sergeant, a corporal, and three privates as a nucleus for a marine corps. The sergeant, George P. Canning, strangely enough appeared to be actually a native of the Southern States. In fact, he represented himself as having been an aide-de-camp to the Confederate general Leonidas Polk. He had been invalided out of the army, he said, on account of a wound suffered at the Battle of Shiloh, and he had an unhealed wound in his chest to support his story. There were also some natives of New England among the new members of the crew, and it made Captain Waddell smile every time he heard the nasal Yankee twang on board a Confederate man-of-war. "Yankee-Confederates!" the Captain chortled, as the Shenandoah, with a spanking breeze, sped along through the Pacific's blue waters.

CHAPTER ELEVEN

FIRST BLOOD AMONG
THE WHALERS

C APTAIN WADDELL had his course pretty well laid out for him after leaving Melbourne, his letter of instructions suggesting that he should proceed first to the New Zealand whaling ground and thence northerly between the Fiji and New Hebrides Islands to the Caroline group. There were detailed directions as to the best course to pursue through the island-dotted South Seas, and there was a hint that Ponape, also called Ascension Island, in the Carolines was a place of resort for whalers.

During the long delay at Melbourne, however, the news of the cruiser's presence had spread throughout the South Pacific. The whaling fleet accustomed to operating in those waters at that season, usually consisting of about forty vessels, had hastily suspended its work and scattered like a flock of chickens alarmed by a hawk's shadow. Some had taken refuge in neighboring ports, and some had gone on to the Arctic. So after leaving Melbourne, although the Shenandoah sailed along day after day on the suggested course, poking her bow into all the likely places in all that expanse of ocean, never a whaler or any other vessel flying the American flag was sighted. Captain Waddell was disturbed in his mind and discouraged, but the cruiser plowed along on her way.

The days dragged tediously by. The officers sat in the ward-room and grumbled because they were not finding any prizes. The opinion was freely expressed that they should have swung to the eastward by Lord Howe's Island, but Waddell, if he knew of the grumbling, paid no attention to the officers' opinions and held stubbornly to his course northward through the Coral Sea. On February 22 the captain joined the officers in drinking a toast to the anniversary of the inauguration of Jefferson Davis as President of the Confederate States. On the first day of March there was a little excitement when the guns, loaded at Melbourne, were fired to clear them of their charges. The next day there was even more commotion when Engineer McGuffeny and Fireman Robinson were found drunk and it was discovered that somebody had gone through the propeller shaft and tapped a barrel of rum, drawing off fifty gallons. Bulloch was on the sick list for several days, and during his illness there again came up the recurring question of Chew's competence, with more friction between the captain and the officers. Time hung heavily on the hands of officers and men, and no opportunity for an argument was allowed to pass unimproved.

For days the wind held on at the north and east, until the ship had reached almost the meridian of the Three Kings, west of the most northwesterly point of

New Zealand, then there was a favorable shift in the air currents, and the vessel was able to make a more directly northerly course between Fearn and Conway Islands, passing by Fiji, Rotumah, and Ellice. But still no enemy sail was sighted. It was proving a tedious and monotonous voyage. But hardly had Fearn Island been passed than the monotony was suddenly and unpleasantly broken. First there came a succession of unusually violent squalls. Then there swooped down a revolving gale from the northeast which held on for four thrillingly tempestuous days.

"In all of my twenty-three years' service on the seas I have never seen anything to equal this," Captain Waddell exclaimed to Whittle as the Shenandoah, enveloped in mist, was buffeted back and forth day after day. But at the same time the commander found comfort, for the severe hammering given the cruiser by the equatorial storm supplied convincing proof of the stanch construction of the little vessel. During the four days of her roaring trial by tempest her easy motion, stability, and dryness increased the commander's admiration for his craft, and he felt confident that after successfully passing through this ordeal she could be relied on to stand up under any weather that might lie ahead.

Following the storm a dead calm ensued, accompanied by torrential, steady downpours of rain—rain which served to accentuate the enervating tropical heat. "Rain water is mighty wet," the men grumbled the sailors' old complaint as they went wearily about their tasks. But after rolling idly for two days with flapping sails, Waddell grew weary of the blistering atmosphere and the inaction, and on March 21 he ordered steam up and steered north in search of a breeze. The search was rewarded the next day, and then under full sail the Shenandoah flew along to the northward. Early on the morning of the twenty-fourth they sighted Drummond Island dead ahead, and, stopping the engine, they ran sufficiently close to the shore to communicate with the natives who came swarming out in their canoes to trade fruit and fish for tobacco, the only article of civilized merchandise in which they seemed interested. Certainly they had no interest in clothes, for they were all stark naked.

The natives were but recently converted from cannibalism, having made it a part of their religion for generations to devour every one whom they captured or killed. But though they were now a bit more civilized, they were still denominated "cannibals" by most of the Shenandoah's men, who regarded the naked, tattooed, dwarfish savages with a distinct air of uneasy suspicion.

"They might forget they'd been converted," one of the men muttered as he saw their canoes approaching.

Among the crew, however, was an old sailor who announced that he had visited the island years before in an American whaler, it being a favorite resort of such vessels for water and fresh fruit, and this old salt assured his shipmates that all the yelling and gesticulating indicated merely a pacific desire to barter.

"I speak a little of their lingo," he said, and

straightway demonstrated the truth of his claim by
beginning to chatter with the men in the nearest
boat Soon the trading was in full swing under the
supervision of the volunteer interpreter, although the
men did not have much tobacco to spare.

Finding that he had an interpreter aboard, Captain Waddell told him, "Ask them if they have seen
any whalers here recently." There ensued another
torrent of conversation, accompanied by eloquent
gestures, and then the old sailor announced, "They
say there haven't been any here for three months."

Upon receipt of this disquieting news Captain
Waddell gave the order to up anchor and proceed,
and the Shenandoah steamed slowly away, much to
the astonishment of the savages, who were evidently
at a loss to understand what made the ship move
without sail. In cautious curiosity they paddled along
in the wake of the cruiser, intently studying the
bubbling water where the propeller was churning up
the sea. But the mischievous Lee, the officer of the
deck, had an idea.

"Blow the whistle," he signalled to the engine room.
Matt O'Brien obliged with a screaming blast, and
the awe-struck savages beat a pell-mell retreat.

The Equator was crossed on the twenty-sixth, but
there was no celebration this time. In the first place,
there were no neophytes to manhandle. Furthermore,
the men were in no mood for skylarking. They were
now passing out of the South Pacific, where they had
expected so many prizes, and some of the officers did
not hesitate to say that the lack of success had been

due to nothing more than bad management on the part of the skipper. Morale was at a low ebb.

"I don't mind admitting to you," Lining morosely told Whittle, "that, as far as I'm concerned, apathy has taken the place of enthusiasm. All I care for now is to get the cruise over and get off the ship."

The other officers were not so outspoken in their criticism, but confidence in the captain was breaking down as they sailed on day after day without a capture or a chase.

At last, on March 29, sailing before a fine trade wind, the lookout gave the cry, "Sail ahead!" When brought to with a blank cartridge, the stranger proved to be the schooner P. Fiert of Honolulu on a trading voyage among the islands in search of tortoise shell and cocoanut oil. Mason, who went on board to establish her nationality (explaining mendaciously that the Shenandoah was the British cruiser Miami), returned with the interesting information that the master of the schooner reported that they had just left Lea Harbor on Ponape Island in the Carolines, and that four Yankee whalers lay peacefully at anchor there. Waddell immediately laid a course for the Carolines, exuberant at the prospect of such rich booty after so many dull and unprofitable days.

They steered slightly out of their course the next day to take a look at the harbor of Chabrol of Strong Island, which was known to be an habitual place of rendezvous for whalers, but the harbor was empty, and so with all sail set the Shenandoah then steered straight for the Carolines, running smoothly before

153

a fine trade wind. Early on the morning of April 1 the lookout reported land on the port bow, and soon the green hills of Ponape rose on the horizon. Almost immediately, however, the sight of land was blotted out by a dense fog, and so the cruiser cautiously lay to for clearer weather.

Those on the cruiser were in a state of high pitched excitement as they waited there in the obscuring fog. The Honolulu schooner was the only sail they had seen between February 20 and April 1. They were sailing over unfamiliar seas on a hazardous errand, and the monotony and lack of success was wearing on their nerves. Commander Waddell, looking at the date on his calendar, laughed bitterly.

"April 1," he said to Whittle. "It would be a good April Fool joke on us if those whalers in Lea Harbor turned out to be neutrals instead of the New Englanders we think they are."

"Yes, no doubt a very fine joke," agreed Whittle drily, "but I doubt whether I'd enjoy it much."

But the lifting of the mist during the morning put a stop to all such gloomy conjectures. As soon as visibility was restored, the engines were started, and the ship put in boldly, for better or for worse. About ten o'clock, as they steamed slowly shoreward, a boat was observed coming out from a point of land, and when it drew up alongside it was found to have been sent out by one of the whalers. They had mistaken the Shenandoah for an expected United States vessel engaged in a coast survey, and they had come out to welcome their fellow-countrymen. The cruiser had not yet shown her flag, and those on board her said nothing to disabuse the Yankees of their erroneous impression. In the boat was an English pilot, Thomas Harrocke, who offered for a consideration of thirty dollars to guide the ship into the harbor, and he was engaged without further parley and taken on board.

Harrocke was a picturesque and weatherbeaten old beachcomber, a native of Yorkshire, who had been a convict many years before in the Australian penal colony, but who had escaped and then been shipwrecked on Ponape, where he had remained for the past thirteen years. Here he had married a native woman and reared a family, and had largely adopted the manners and customs of the islanders. His body was tattooed with all sorts of fantastic designs, and he had been separated from his English speaking fellows for so long that he now spoke his native language with noticeable hesitation and difficulty. But he knew Lea Harbor like the palm of his hand, and he handled the wheel with the skill of an oldtimer as he put the Shenandoah carefully across the reef which guarded the harbor.

Meanwhile the cruiser still raised no flag. Waddell volunteered no information as to her nationality, and Harrocke asked no questions. Waddell had unbent to the extent of telling him that if the Shenandoah did not reach the anchorage safely, he would be held personally responsible, and the commander, wearing his arms, stood by Harrocke's side as he eased her through the channel and into the bay where peacefully lay at anchor the four Yankee whalers, the Harvest, the Pearl, the Hector, and the Edmund Cary.

Safely inside, the cruiser was hove to and anchored in fifteen fathoms of water between the reef and a rock dangerously located in midchannel, and to hold her steadily in position and to prevent any dangerous drift in the currents, Captain Waddell had lines run out from her sides and made fast to trees on the shore. Then, when he had finally got the ship anchored to his satisfaction, four boats were lowered to the water, the port and starboard whaleboats and the second and third cutters, commanded by Grimball, Chew, Lee, and Scales. The boats were of moderate proportions, about thirty feet long and six feet in the beam, but they were strongly built, and each carried in addition to the lieutenant a petty officer and a prize crew of seven men, all armed with cutlasses and revolvers.

While all this was going on, the whalers, in honor of the visit of the supposed American cruiser, had proudly run their colors up to their peaks, and soon the Stars and Stripes fluttered brightly at the mastheads against the dark green background of the tropical foliage. But to their dismay, as soon as her four boats were well on their way to their respective victims, the Shenandoah hoisted the Confederate flag and fired a blank shell to emphasize the fact that the April Fool joke was on the New England skippers. The booming gun re-echoed among the tropical hills, and the natives who had gathered on the beach to stare at the visitor took prompt and precipitate refuge in the dense undergrowth. The whalers accepted the situation with a complacency born of necessity and hauled down their flags as the boarding parties clambered on their decks.

Harrocke, who had been regaling some of the cruiser's officers and men with hair-raising stories of his experiences during his long residence among the savages, was as surprised as anybody when the Confederate flag was raised. It was a strange piece of bunting to him.

"What the hell flag is that?"

"That," answered Minor, relishing the opportunity to impress the old derelict, "is the flag of the Confederate States of America."

Somewhat to their surprise, they learned that the old Englishman was not entirely ignorant of what this signified. He had a vague understanding of the fact that there was a big war in progress in America. Some of the trading vessels visiting the island had told him about it, he said. And he added, with crude diplomacy, that they had told him that in all the big battles the Southerners had whipped the Yankees— all of which the Shenandoah's officers gravely confirmed.

"Well, well, I never thought I'd live to see Jeff Davis's flag." And, looking up at the snapping bunting, he added, "It's pretty. It looks like the English white flag."

Then, while the boarding crews were taking charge of the whalers, Harrocke gave the Confederate visitors a sketchy account of the Caroline Islands and the habits of the native tribes. He had been in imminent peril of his life when he first was cast up on that savage shore, he said, but he had been successful in persuading the natives to regard him as a friend and a being of superior endowments instead of looking upon him as something to be added to their menu. With all his ups and downs, he seemed well satisfied with his lot and expressed no desire to return to civilization.

"It's a bit lonely out here," he said, "but it's jolly."

There was one other white man on the islands, Harrocke told them, a missionary from Massachusetts. It appeared, however, that the missionary had been occupying himself principally in an effort to turn an honest penny by trading in tortoise shell, and some of the practices in which he engaged in his business dealings with the natives were of such a character as to shake their faith in the principles of morality to which he had tried to convert them. As a result, the natives remained unregenerate, and the Massachusetts divine was getting rich. And so thoroughly was he engrossed in his preaching or in his trading that he never showed himself while the Shenandoah was there.

Soon the four boats returned from the captive vessels, each rowed by one of the petty officers, the lieutenant and armed crew in each instance being left in charge of the captured whaler. The boarding officers had been ordered particularly to send back from each vessel its officers, papers, log books, navigating instruments, and charts. The last were deemed of especial importance, as it had not been possible to supply the Shenandoah with the particular type of charts used by the whalers, those showing every track and where previous expeditions had been most successful in taking whales. With these charts now in his possession, Captain Waddell felt that he held the key to the navigation of all the Pacific Islands, the Okhotsk and Bering Seas, and the Arctic Ocean, and also that he possessed information which would be helpful to him in locating the great Arctic whaling fleet of New England without a blind and time-wasting search.

The only respect in which the boarding crews fell short of carrying out their instructions was that they were not able to send back the captains of the four whalers. The first and second mates of each were in the returning boats, but the captains had gone ashore "for a merry-making" with the missionary, and were not expected back until some time late in the evening.

About sunset the errant captains returned to the harbor from their jollification on shore. When the strange and unwelcome sight of the cruiser in the harbor flying the Confederate flag first burst on their view, they rested on their oars in obvious astonishment. Quickly then, as they realized the situation, they put about and pulled back frantically for the shore, but the Shenandoah's boat soon overhauled them, and they were captured and conducted to the deck of the cruiser for questioning by the commander. Their surprise and dismay was increased when they found their officers and crews held prisoners on the Confederate vessel, but they submitted more or less gracefully to their fate. The captains of the Edward Cary, the Hector, and the Pearl frankly admitted that they could give no good reason why they should not permit themselves to be made prisoners. The captain of the Harvest raised a vague and feeble protest to the effect that his vessel had been transferred to the flag of the Sandwich Islands, but he could produce no bill of sale substantiating this claim, and since she bore the name "Harvest of New Bedford" on her side, carried an American register, and was admittedly in charge of the same American captain who had commanded her on former voyages, Waddell decided against the credibility of the captain's story and condemned her to the same fate as her companions.

The master of the Hector proved to be somewhat more truculent than the others. He had been engaged in the work of blocking the harbor of Charleston in 1861, when the stone-laden vessels were sunk in the channel there, and he loudly and vociferously boasted of the damage he had done the Confederate cause on that occasion.

"I calculate we just about ruined that harbor," he crowed, "and I only hope to live to do the rebels as much damage again some day. You can burn my ship if you want to, you damned pirate. I can't stop you. But you and Jeff Davis and all the other damned traitors will stew in Hell before it's all over."

Loudly and excitedly he abused the Confederate cause and all those who fought on that side. At last, growing weary of the Yankee's frenzied tirade, Captain Waddell warned him to desist. But he persisted in his abuse, and the captain finally ordered him put in double irons and gagged until his fury subsided.

On the other hand, the captain of the Pearl proved unexpectedly friendly. Although a New Englander himself, he boasted a Virginia mother, and willingly volunteered information about the regions in the North Pacific where the whaling fleet would probably be found.

The remainder of the afternoon was spent in transferring some of the stores from the captured vessels to the Shenandoah, and when night fell Captain Waddell retired to his cabin with a feeling of exultation at the fortunate outcome of his April Fool's Day raid. The four vessels were valued collectively at more than $100,000, aside from the value of their stores. In addition, he had obtained from his prizes the whaling charts he so sorely needed. It was the Shenandoah's first really rich haul.

That very day Commander Rodgers of the U. S. S. Iroquois was officially notifying Secretary Welles at Washington that he had just arrived in Batavia Roads, Island of Java, where he hoped soon to find the Shenandoah. The next day Commander Townsend of the U. S. S. Wachusett reported to Welles from St. Pierre, Martinique, that he was lying in wait for the Shenandoah at that point and expected to find her almost any day. At the same time, Commander Shirley of the U. S. S. Suwanee was reporting his arrival at Bahia, Brazil, pursuing a report that the Shenandoah had just been seen in that neighborhood.

CHAPTER TWELVE

DIPLOMACY *A LA* CANNIBAL

———————

THE SECOND DAY of April, 1865, was a bleak day in the history of the Southern Confederacy. In the misty early hours of that showery Sunday Grant's irresistible pressure broke Lee's thin line in front of Petersburg, and a few hours later the Stars and Bars were pulled down for the last time from the flagpole of the capitol at Richmond. That day Richmond was evacuated. President Davis and his Cabinet took flight, and within a week Lee surrendered to Grant at Appomattox.

But six thousand miles away, on a tiny speck of an island in the South Pacific, a quite different scene was being staged that fateful Sunday morning. There the flag of the Confederate States was flying in proud triumph from the masthead of the Shenandoah as she lay in Lea Harbor, and the ship's officers, flushed with gratification, were gathered on deck in their best bibs and tuckers to receive an official visit from Ish-y-paw, the king of the cannibal islands.

Elated with his easy capture of the four Yankee whalers at one swoop, Commander Waddell felt inclined to take a little time out for the purpose of

observing the amenities due the sovereign of the little
island whose guests they were. Accordingly, on the
morning of the second he sent the gig ashore in command of Hunt to bring King Ish-y-paw and his retinue aboard the Shenandoah to be officially received
by the commander of the cruiser in the name of the
Confederate States of America.

Hunt was accompanied ashore by six armed sailors
and the interpreter, Harrocke, all very much impressed with the importance of their mission. As they
approached the beach, however, it quickly became
apparent that the natives were not acquainted with
the pacific nature of their visit, for as the gig was
pulled through the foaming combers, they encountered a gesticulating multitude of savages, armed
with stones and brandishing their native knives fashioned from sharks' teeth. But Hunt urged Harrocke to acquaint the warriors with their friendly in-
tentions, and as soon as this was made clear to them,
the natives laid aside their weapons and hospitably
helped them beach the gig and disembark.

The king that day was not in his accustomed royal
hut near the beach, but was at another of his official
residences further inland. Two of the native chiefs
volunteered to conduct Hunt and Harrocke to the
king's domicile, not without certain misgivings on
the part of Hunt, who thought he detected on the
faces of some of the cannibal escort an unsatisfied
appetite for white meat. After scrambling laboriously
over a rough path through the jungle, they eventually reached the rude palace, a large but flimsy
structure of bamboo, with high roof and low eaves,

163

in which sat the king, surrounded by some three hundred of his subjects, all armed, engaged in a native celebration.

The king was seated on his throne, a platform of bamboo raised a few inches above the floor, and as Hunt and Harrocke were brought into his august presence he rose to greet them. The king was almost a pigmy, barely five feet high, and his only article of clothing aside from a collar and an embroidered belt was a scanty little apron made of grass. As an ornament he wore a large clay pipe thrust through a hole in the lobe of his ear, and for protection against the mosquitoes, he was smeared with a thick coating of rancid cocoanut oil, the smell of which struck his white visitors like a blow.

With due formality Hunt was presented to the king by Harrocke, and the king made his visitor welcome by asking to examine his sword and pistol. Having satisfied his curiosity, he invited his honored guest to join him in a bumper of *gorwa*, a native species of liquid dynamite. When these formalities had been completed, Hunt was permitted to state the object of his visit, which he did with suitable flourishes. The king appeared to be a little coy about accepting the invitation to go on board the cruiser, but Hunt was courteously insistent, and so the king annointed his royal body with another coating of the malodorous oil and announced that he was ready to visit the white chief.

The visit displayed the pomp becoming to a reigning monarch. The king was accompanied by the hereditary prince and four of his principal chieftains, each attired in the apron of sea grass and each wearing a wreath of flowers around his brow. They were given the seats of honor in the gig, Hunt prudently taking a seat in the bow where he could not smell his passengers, and as the boat was pulled out to the Shenandoah, they were followed at a respectful distance by a swarming fleet of nearly a hundred native canoes, each carrying from three to five natives and all gaudily decorated in honor of the occasion.

Captain Waddell outdid himself in preparing a welcome for the visiting king, but Ish-y-paw's actual arrival on the deck of the cruiser was not without an unfortunate element of low comedy.

The commander stood at the head of the accommodation ladder in full regalia and smiling graciously as the king came up slowly and cautiously, feeling his way with great care in his unfamiliar surroundings. Arrived at the rail, he carefully straightened his apron and calmly seated himself between the headboards of the gangway and waited expectantly. The position he took effectively blocked the progress of the hereditary prince, who was still hanging desperately to a manrope on the side of the vessel, and this in turn held Harrocke in the gig. Since Harrocke was the only available interpreter, the king-guest and the commander-host were in a conversational cul-desac at the head of the gangway, but the trying moment which might have been prolonged into an embarrassing diplomatic episode was cut abruptly short by a sudden roll of the vessel which threw the king onto the deck in a most unregal state of confusion.

The occupants of the gig were then able to come on board, and by the time the king had pulled himself erect, his retinue was gathered about him, and Harrocke had come forward to do the honors as interpreter.

It developed, however, that Harrocke had only the faintest idea of the official formalities of international relations, and he introduced the visiting monarch by the simple device of nodding his head in the direction of the regal presence and saying casually to Waddell, "That's the king, sir." The commander acknowledged the introduction with what he considered the proper degree of formal deference and invited the whole party into his cabin, where he ceremoniously proffered his guests the choicest vintages from the ship's rather limited wine cellar.

The king, however, turned up his royal nose at the wine, whereupon one of the petty officers remarked in a grim aside that his cannibalistic majesty would probably prefer "a slice of cold roast Confederate." But Commander Waddell was prepared for all tastes, so he produced tobacco and a bottle of Schiedam schnapps, and of these the visitors partook liberally. Indeed, Ish-y-paw displayed an astonishing capacity for schnapps and tossed off several bumpers of the fiery liquid, gulping it down greedily between puffs at his pipe.

While thus engaged he beckoned to the interpreter and whispered something in his ear. Harrocke listened attentively and then gravely interpreted.

"He says he wants to spit, but don't like to spit on the carpet!"

Touched by this display of unexpected gentility, the captain called a sailor who quickly produced a wooden box filled with sand, and King Ish-y-paw was then able to smoke and drink and spit to his royal heart's content as, mellowed by the schnapps, he breathed out expressions of great friendship for his honorable visitors. At last the king arose and announced the visit at an end, and he and his staff solemnly climbed down over the side and departed, promising a return visit on the following day.

All this attention to the little king was not frivolous and purposeless on Captain Waddell's part. He had serious work at hand in disposing of the captured whalers, and he wished if possible to make his plans with the native ruler's consent and co-operation, giving them all possible color of legality. Cordially he greeted the king next day when he returned with his princes and his chiefs for another visit. Again the tobacco and schnapps were passed around, and when everybody was feeling comfortably mellow, the commander proceeded, through Harrocke, to explain to the king the reason why a Confederate warship was present in his harbor.

"The history and character of the war," the commander said with utmost solemnity, "I shall not go into. They are so familiar to your majesty as not to require repetition."

His majesty grunted and took another glass of schnapps.

"These ships here," Waddell waved his arm in a sweeping gesture in the direction of the whalers, "belong to my country's enemies, people who have been hostile to us for forty years and will be always so until the end of time, people who have wronged us in every conceivable way for nearly half a century and have climaxed their record of enmity by invading and pillaging our country."

When Harrocke put this into Carolinese, the king manifested his comprehension simply.

"You don't like one another."

Waddell agreed that this was the general idea he sought to convey and proceeded, with Harrocke translating phrase by phrase.

"No," Waddell said, "it is incompatible with virtue that the South should ever be reconciled to the North again. Blood has been spilt. Life has been taken. Our countrywomen have been outraged, and the unprotected have been driven into the forest for shelter while their homes are destroyed by fire. I am ordered to capture and destroy their vessels whenever it shall be within my power to do so, and if your majesty's laws of neutrality [here his majesty looked confused] would not be violated, I will confiscate the vessels in port. As there is very little in them which this steamer requires, I propose to present their contents to your majesty, which you can make use of as you wish, and when your tribe have finished with them I will take them to sea and burn them."

When Waddell had finished this harangue, the king and his staff held a short council, at the conclusion of which he told the commander that they found nothing conflicting with their native laws in what he proposed to do. Placated by the promise of plunder, the king even went so far as to point out some con-

venient shoals onto which the doomed whalers could
be run for burning. His only request was that the
cruiser refrain from firing any guns at the whaling
vessels, for fear that someone on shore might be hurt.
To this Waddell graciously consented, as he did not
intend to do it anyway. The king and his retinue
withdrew, and the first and only diplomatic parley
between the Confederate States of America and the
ruler of the Caroline Islands was brought to a satis-
factory end.

These diplomatic proceedings having been completed, the work of destruction began. First the
Harvest was brought alongside the Shenandoah and
her supply of fresh water and provisions was transferred to the captor vessel. The cruiser also took on
board the five tons of sperm oil found on the Harvest,
and some of the stores found aboard. Among these
latter were seventy "down East" muskets, an unre-
liable type of firearm manufactured in New England
expressly for trading with the South Sea islanders,
and two dozen infantry uniforms, which Waddell
was glad to have for the purpose of uniforming the
marine corps he was trying to organize. He also removed from the other vessels such articles as might
be of value to the Shenandoah, after first permitting
the officers and members of the crews to remove such
of their personal belongings as they wished to save.
The whalers were then run onto the shoals, and the
king was notified that the natives might go through
them at their pleasure and take anything and everything they wished.

Before this wholesale looting began, however,

Waddell pointed out to the king that the Shenandoah was riding in a more or less dangerous position at her anchorage between the reef and the rock, and that if any wicked person on shore should cut the hawsers tied to the trees which held the cruiser in position, a shift in the wind might easily drive the vessel aground. He made it plain to the king that the "wicked persons" he had in mind were not any of the natives but some of the members of the whalers' crews who had discreetly jumped overboard and swum ashore when they first saw the Confederate flag raised on the cruiser.

"Now, what I desire your majesty to do is to station some of your warriors to guard the fasts, with orders to shoot anyone who goes within certain prescribed limits."

The king readily enough accepted this proposal in theory, but he pointed out one practical objection.

"I have the warriors," he said affably, "but they can not shoot anyone. I have no muskets nor ammunition."

Waddell knew that there were no firearms on the island, and he also knew that the savages delighted in the possession of such weapons. So he presented the king with the seventy muskets and a supply of ammunition, and Ish-y-paw agreed to guard the fasts as requested. Waddell privately expressed the fervent hope that none of the natives would have occasion to fire one of the weapons before the departure of the Shenandoah.

"I would prefer the muzzle to the chamber of one of those cheap-john Yankee muskets."

But the savages were extremely proud of their new guns, and were just as delighted with them as though they had been the latest model army rifles. The gratified king declared himself secure from any possible harm now that he was provided with such a splendid arsenal.

The natives, once they were turned loose on the doomed whalers, made the most of this windfall of unrestrained looting. All that day, and the next day and the next, they swarmed over the vessels. Their canoes, constantly passing to and fro between the ships and the shore, excited the admiration of the warship's crew by the skill and dexterity with which they were handled, and the sailors enjoyed the affair just about as much as the laughing, chattering savages.

Every movable plank, spar, and bulkhead was ripped from the ships and taken on shore for use in flooring the native huts. The sails were removed from the yards and sail-rooms for their own canoes and for tents. Even the copper was stripped from the vessels' bottoms, copper being a highly-prized metal among the natives for pointing arrows and spears, for making breastplates and shields, and for trading with other tribes. Then there was the ships' bread and tobacco, odd bits of iron, harpoons and whaling lines. The natives must have handed down stories for many generations of that glorious time when they were permitted to plunder until they were weary of plundering.

Meanwhile the king and the commander were getting along most handsomely, drinking schnapps and exchanging gifts and assurances of mutual esteem. The king, in token of his appreciation of all the schnapps he was consuming, daily sent aboard presents of fish and fresh fruit. Waddell presented him with a silk scarf, which he greatly admired, and the king sent the captain a belt woven by some of his people out of the fibres of the cocoanut interwoven with bright strands of wool. This gaudy trophy, the commander assured him, he would forever cherish "as a memento of the only sovereign who had the independence of character and fearlessness of disposition to perform a common duty toward a righteous people and just cause."

This speech touched the king's heart, and he showed his regard for his guest by spontaneously and generously making him a present of the royal princess. Waddell, being already married, felt impelled to decline the dusky damsel, rude though his refusal might be considered, and the interpreter had some difficulty in making it clear to the king why so luscious a gift was rejected on such purely technical grounds.

Ish-y-paw was not offended, however, and to show his further interest in his visitors requested that he and his staff might be permitted to inspect the steamer throughout. Waddell of course assented, and in honor of the occasion formally presented the king with the sword which had been found aboard the Charter Oak several months before.

Ish-y-paw had never seen a sword before Waddell's visit and did not exactly understand its use or purpose, but Waddell assured him that a sword was an essential feature of every true king's equipment, and also that it might prove of value to him in the future. With some reluctance he was persuaded to belt it to his naked waist, swinging it on his right side, to the amusement of all the officers, but he eyed the weapon suspiciously and seemed to entertain some doubt of the propriety of having it so near his royal person. Waddell, however, insisted that it was absolutely necessary.

All went well until the party began descending to the engine room. The sword became entangled in the king's legs and precipitated him into an undignified sprawl. Hereupon, despite all protestations, Ish-y-paw firmly insisted on divesting himself of the sword, and throughout the rest of the tour the hereditary prince carried the weapon gingerly in his arms. The king was then able to derive unrestrained enjoyment from looking at the machinery, manifesting his pleasure and wonder by repeated clucks of the tongue, which were re-echoed by his admiring staff.

Not to be outdone in hospitality, before departing from the Shenandoah King Ish-y-paw extended to Commander Waddell an invitation to visit him ashore at his royal residence. The commander accepted the invitation, and the next day went ashore with his suite to pay the formal visit. A prince met him and his party when they landed on the beach and conducted them to the temporary palace, which was perched on six piles near the margin of the harbor above reach of the flood tide.

The palace was a hut of one room measuring six by eight feet, built of canes interlaced with vines, and roofed with the broad leaves of the cocoanut, with a pair of rickety steps leading to the door. In this tiny house the royal family ate, slept, and received their visitors. The king, upon Waddell's arrival, was seated on his royal bed, a straw mat folded in the corner, and his queen was sitting on the floor near him, her hands and chin resting on her knees. Neither rose to greet the visitor, but the king motioned him to a seat on a battered old trunk, evidently the place of honor.

During the course of the visit the king casually asked Waddell what method would be used in putting his prisoners to death, taking it for granted that this was the proper disposition of one's captive enemies. Waddell explained loftily that in civilized warfare it was customary to kill only those who were in armed resistance and to parole the unarmed.

"But," objected the king with sound though savage logic, "war is not civilized, and people who make war are bad people and ought to be killed."

Waddell had no good answer for this, but could merely reiterate the virtuous position taken by the self-styled civilized nations. The king thought this very noble, and in token of his admiration gave the commander two chickens and a basket of fruit to take home to Jeff Davis with his compliments.

"Jeff Davis must be a good man," the king pronounced.

While the captain was thus fraternizing with the king, the officers were spending their time in sightseeing trips ashore, like tourists in a new country. Whittle and three of the others got out their fowling pieces and went gunning for plover. Dr. Lining went sailing on the bay in the whale-boat and broke his best pair of eyeglasses. In various detachments all the officers went around the island to view the mysterious stone ruins on the islets of Nan-Matal and Nan-Tauach, immense fortifications with bastions built up of huge prisms of basalt weighing tons, mute evidence of an abandoned civilization of centuries ago. One party paid a social call on the king's sister, Susannah Banana, who hospitably entertained them by showing them her elaborate tattoos. Some of the men were so highly pleased with this display of cutaneous art that they had similar designs tattooed on their own bodies, the work being done by one of the old women of the island who used the sharp prongs of a thorn tree and a native dye.

At last, however, the Shenandoah's work in this quarter was completed. The natives had stripped the whalers of everything of value, and they had been burned to the waterline in what must have been the most spectacular bonfire ever witnessed in that part of the world. Seven members of the whalers' crews had enlisted with the Shenandoah, three seamen, three landsmen, and a third-class boy, and the rest of the prisoners were given their choice of being held on the cruiser to be landed on Guam or left on Ponape. They chose the latter course, and permission having been granted by Ish-y-paw to leave them there, they were set ashore with their personal effects, ample provisions, and two whaleboats, to await some casual vessel of rescue to take them back to civilization.

So, wrote Commander Waddell grimly in his log,

"The morning of the 13th of April saw all prisoners clear of the steamer, and at noon she tripped her anchors and stood to sea, leaving to the care of the king and his tribe 130 disappointed whalers, who had been accustomed to ill-treat the natives and cheat them, besides introducing loathsome diseases never till then known to the tribes. That harbor will always be one of interest to the Yankee whalers, and tradition will point out the exact shoals on which the prizes were burned and where the Shenandoah lay calmly at anchor amid that scene of vengeance and destruction."

In faraway Greensboro, North Carolina, on April 13 General Joseph E. Johnston was writing a letter to General Sherman proposing a suspension of hostilities "to enter into the needful arrangements to terminate the existing war"—the prelude to his surrender a few days later. Four days previously, on April 9, he had surrendered to Grant at Appomatox. The Southern Confederacy was crumbling into dust. But blissfully ignorant of all this, Waddell set sail for the North Pacific seeking more whalers to conquer.

CHAPTER THIRTEEN

FROM THE TROPICS
TO THE ICE

ACROSS THE NORTH PACIFIC there lay, in the days of the clipper ships, a broad two-way highway frequented by the vessels operating in the China trade. Those bound from San Francisco to Hong Kong kept pretty close to the path lying between the parallels of 17° and 20° north latitude, because the trade wind there is at its best. The track for ships from the China coast to California was between 39° and 45°, those being the latitudes where the west winds prevail. It was to this much traveled Hong Kong path that Captain Waddell turned the Shenandoah's prow after leaving Ponape, hoping to fall in with some of the rich merchantmen trading between California and the Orient.

It was a ten days' cruise from Ponape to the northern highway, and it was ten days of perfect weather. A bright sun by day and a full moon by night lighted up the broad face of the Pacific as the slim cruiser, with full sail set, plowed steadily to the northward. The boatswain and his helpers busied themselves in petty repairs about the ship, but most of the now ample crew had little to do but loll on deck and bask in the never-ending sunshine.

The officers, too, found time hanging heavily on their hands. They had played so much chess and whist that they were temporarily fed up with games, but Chew got out his fiddle and the irrepressible Lee entertained the others with a comic dance which set the wardroom to roaring with laughter. They shouted demands for encores until the dancer was exhausted. The stay ashore at Melbourne had served to relax some of the tension which had grown up during the preceding weeks, and the young men were now getting along well together again, joking and teasing each other as they had at the beginning of the cruise. Grimball and Lining, who both came from South Carolina, engaged in endless detailed conversations about their common friends and acquaintances among the families along the Southern seaboard until they became the butt of a lot of good-natured teasing from the others.

"Wait a minute there," one would interrupt, "I've got Ralph Elliott mixed up with Montmorency."

"Yes," chimed in Whittle, "and I want to know why Ethel Newcome didn't marry Thomas Rhett. I thought last week she surely would."

But although they teased each other and skylarked, there was one subject, deadly serious, on which they all seemed to agree, and that was criticism of the captain. When all other subjects of conversation failed, they could always come back to this.

"Why doesn't he lay a course for Guam?" asked

Lining. "That's where the whalers go, and I happen to know he's expected to go there."

But Waddell held to his northward course, and there was nothing to disturb the serenity of life aboard the cruiser except an occasional fight in the steerage which sent one of the surgeons hurrying below to sew up a split scalp or poultice a bashed-in nose.

The first of May found the Shenandoah fairly in the track of the North Pacific clippers, and the lookouts on their lofty perches in the rigging swept the sea with watchful eyes, but all to no purpose. It seemed as though all the rich merchantmen had had a premonition of the presence of the Confederate raider. At any rate, there were none to be found, although Captain Waddell kept weaving about the accustomed paths of the China ships. So after several disappointing days of fruitless cruising, passing and repassing league after league of the great maritime highway, the captain decided to abandon that unproductive hunting ground and to stand to the northward once more. They had not had a glimpse of a sail since leaving Ponape, and the conscientious Waddell was anxious to be about his duty of destruction.

Headed northward, Captain Waddell's concern over his inexplicable failure to encounter fish for his net was complicated by a new source of worry. The further north the ship proceeded, the more unfavorable the weather became, and by the time he reached the parallel 43° it had grown increasingly cold and foggy. The winds were westerly, but unsteady in force, and the captain, with increasing alarm, watched the telltale barometer, which indicated an impending change. Warned by the falling pressure, he prudently put his little ship in the best possible shape to stand up under whatever evil forces might be forthcoming, and then resolutely waited.

Gradually the signs of ugly weather increased. The surface of the sea boiled and bubbled like a rip tide. The sun was now blotted out by the lowering skies. Soon there approached from the northeast a sinister black cloud, lying so closely upon the surface of the water that it threatened to engulf and extinguish the little vessel which stood so stanchly in its path. There was a menacing quality in the very atmosphere, a threat which though intangible was positively and oppressively present. The men, their preparation done, stood silent on the deck in fearful expectancy, as though cringing before an impending blow. The dark cloud rolled on toward them inexorably. There was a puff of a breeze, warm and unnatural, and then a drumming spatter of rain-drops.

"A typhoon, Mr. Whittle," warned the Captain simply, and hardly had he uttered the words before the storm struck in full fury, howling down on the pitching cruiser like some vengeful demon.

The ship staggered before that first fierce gust and careened over until the ends of her lower yards were drenched by the spray of the rapidly rising sea. Then, recovering from her first shock, she righted herself almost immediately, shook the black water from her strong white wings, nodded her head as though in defiance of the storm, and scudded off before the screaming gale like something alive.

Throughout the rest of the night the storm bore down with unrelenting force. When daylight came the wind was at its height, carrying the ship along at twelve knots, with close-reefed fore-topsail and reefed foresail. Preventer braces were got aloft, hatches battened down, and so far as was possible everything was done to insure the vessel's safety. Boatswain Harwood was everywhere at once, never sleeping and never tiring. He was a veteran of the British navy, with a vast knowledge of the sea and its ways gained from twenty years before the mast. It gave both the inexperienced young officers and the crew a feeling of reassurance to see the air of competence and confidence with which he went about his duties.

Hour after hour the typhoon blew with no visible ill effect on the ship. Perhaps she might ride it out unscathed. But suddenly, with a noise like a cannon, the main-topsail broke from the leech ropes and flew away before the wind, blown into shreds and flapping wildly in the rigging.

There was but one thing to do in such an emergency. It was desperate, risky business, but a new sail must be bent, typhoon or no typhoon. Promptly the officer of the deck ordered the main-topmen aloft to secure such remnants of the sail as were still attached to the yards, flailing the air like giant whips. The sailors sprang to their dangerous duty, and for endless minutes the rest of the crew on deck watched their painful progress in the shrouds as they inched their way upward, matching their strength against the typhoon. At times they were held immovable against the rigging by the sheer force of the wind.

Then slowly they would creep upward again, cling-
ing desperately to the shrouds as the wind roared
about them and the pelting rain lashed savagely at
them. At last they reached the yard, and then coolly
but cautiously made their way out onto it. As the
ship rolled in the heavy seas, the yard would point
one minute to the heavens, and the next would be directed at the depths on the opposite side. But the
men clung on by some miracle of strength and agility,
and proceeded with incredible skill and courage to
remove what remained of the tattered sail and put the
new canvas in place, secured and sheeted home, and
then close-reefed by means of the revolving yard.

When at last the main-topmen had returned to the
deck, an extra round of grog was served in honor of
their accomplishment. But hardly had the men
stopped smacking their lips before a new peril im-
pended. For hours the seas had been running high,
covering the decks with splashing spray. Without
warning, there came crashing over the bows a gi-
gantic wave, like a collapsing cliff of water, filling
the deck to the waist and sending the surprised men
floundering into the scuppers. For the second time
since leaving Funchal the ports had to be knocked
out to free the vessel of the tremendous volume of
water which threatened to founder her by its sheer
weight. Then, as the water poured out through the
ports and the men were recovering themselves from
their drenching and their fright, another great wall
of water came rolling over the trembling ship. As it
swept across the deck, it caught one man unprepared
and carried him screaming overboard. But by a

miracle of tempestuous perversity, the terrified sailor was the next moment dashed back on deck by another heavy sea, scared out of his wits, his teeth chattering, but otherwise uninjured.

The ship was now beginning to roll so heavily that the royal yards were sent down on deck and secured in the fore, main, and mizzen rigging. All that day the vessel rushed before the terrific force of the wind. When the gale began to die down at nightfall, it had carried the ship westward more than a hundred miles out of her course. The gale was succeeded by a steady torrent of rain which drenched everybody to the skin, but the Shenandoah was now able to make her northing again, and the sailors congratulated themselves that the heavy rain would help beat down the high seas and give them smoother sailing. The typhoon was blowing itself out after trying the stanchness of the ship and the courage of the men as nothing had ever before tried either.

By May 17 the ship was north of the forty-fifth parallel. The weather, though now decidedly colder, looked more settled, and everybody felt more hopeful as the cruiser shaped her course northward for the Amphitrite Straits which formed the entrance to the Okhotsk Sea.

On the twentieth there rose into view the snowy summits of the mountainous Kuril Islands, and this sight served as a renewed reminder to the men on board that the days of pleasant weather were now behind them and that snow and ice would be their portion for weeks and months to come. Chests and clothesbags were ransacked for woollen underclothing. Heavy peajackets and overcoats were dragged out, and all possible preparations were made for the frigid days ahead of them.

It was at this time that Dr. Lining and his assistant, Dr. McNulty, made their value to the expedition most keenly felt. Backed up by the captain, they insisted on the observation of a strict regime for the prevention of sickness. The men, it was ordered, must keep themselves warmly clad and dry at all times. Extra rations of grog and hot coffee were served at regular hours throughout the entire stay of the cruiser in northern waters, and Dr. McNulty carefully inspected every meal for the crew before and after it was prepared. The best possible precautions were taken for keeping the vessel sanitary, and thanks to the vigilance of Lining and McNulty, there was not a serious case of illness on board at any time while the ship was in high latitudes despite the rigorous weather encountered.

Within twenty days the Shenandoah had run from the tropics into snow and ice, from excessive heat to excessive cold, but the members of the crew in their heavy pea jackets only laughed as they gazed at the snow on the Kurils and looked forward with eager anticipation to their invasion of the Arctic Circle.

But there was less laughter now among the officers as their distrust of the captain mounted. Chew, coming off his watch, disdainfully reported Waddell's skittery nervousness as they steamed into the straits.

" 'Make haste, Mr. Chew,' he says to me as we were cleaving up the topsails. 'I don't want to go on shore here!' 'Go on shore' although we are under

steam and the shore is four miles off. How could we
go on shore? What's the matter with him? Has he lost
his nerve?"

"Well," said Lining, always glad to chime in when
the captain was under attack, "we're too far off the
coast, if you ask me. Everybody knows that the
whalers hunt close in—that is, everybody but the
captain knows it."

And there was an extended discussion of the skipper's shortcomings as a commander and a navigator
which provided food for hours of conversation.

Hardly had this flurry of grousing subsided before the captain gave the young officers further cause
for censure. Scales came down sick, and the unpredictable captain, to everyone's surprise, announced
that he would take Scales' watch. Superconscientious,
Waddell leaned backward in his anxiety to share the
hardship, but the officers did not understand or appreciate that quality in him.

"It looks bad for the skipper to be standing a
watch when he has two lieutenants who could do it
instead of him," Bulloch complained to Dr. Lining.
But Lining was ready with a surprising explanation.

"He told me not long ago he thought the worry
of the cruise would drive him crazy. Maybe it has."

"Well, I wouldn't say he's crazy," said Bulloch
cautiously, "but he does some curious things. Why,
on the Alabama—"

The wardroom gossip droned on as the "Shenanigan" slipped past the bleak islands of the Kuril
group with snow sifting down softly on her decks.

CHAPTER FOURTEEN

CHASING WHALERS IN
THE FLOES

ON THE NIGHT of May 26 the Shenandoah passed through the Amphitrite Straits and, with the lofty snowclad mountains of Kamchatka looming bleak and barren on the starboard bow, steamed into the Sea of Okhotsk, where it was thought likely some of the whalers would be found.

The very next day about noon a sail was sighted by the lookout, but owing to the intervention of field ice it was late in the afternoon before the stranger could be reached. Standing along close to the western margin of the field ice until she had rounded its northern point, the cruiser raised the Russian ensign to her masthead, to which the whaler responded with the Stars and Stripes. The Confederate flag was then raised on the Shenandoah, a warning shot was fired from the twelve-pounder, and the Abigail of New Bedford hove to.

Hunt was sent with a crew to board the whaler. When he formally announced to Captain Nye that he was a prisoner to the Confederate cruiser Shenandoah, the old Yankee looked at him in astonishment, took a fresh chew of tobacco, and then calmly remarked:

"Well, I s'pose I'm taken. But who on earth would have thought of seeing one of you rebels' boats away up here in the Okhotsk? I supposed I was out of your reach."

Hunt was feeling a bit facetious that afternoon.

"Why, the fact of the business is, Captain, that we have entered into an offensive and defensive treaty with the whales, and we are up here by special agreement to disperse their mortal enemies."

"All right, my boy. I never grumble at what I can't help. But the whales needn't owe me much of a grudge, for the Lord knows I haven't disturbed 'em much this voyage, though I've done my part at blubber-hunting in years gone by. But," he added hospitably, "it's cold talking out here. Come below and take something to warm your stomach while I get my papers"—a suggestion to which the obliging Hunt made no objection.

For the most part the crew, like the captain, accepted their capture with complacent good humor, and one of them as he came over the side remarked gravely to a grinning Confederate sailor, "Well, I hadn't expected to take steam home, and, to tell the truth, I had just as lief trust to sail. But anyhow I'll try it with you and see how I like it."

When Captain Nye came on board and was interrogated by Waddell, it developed that this was not an unique experience for him. Early in the war he had fallen into the hands of Admiral Semmes and had his vessel destroyed, and he had gone into the whaling trade with the deliberate and avowed intent of removing himself from the war's dangers.

The Abigail had been thriftily fitted out with the idea of doing some trading as well as whaling, and for that purpose was carrying about fifty barrels of whiskey. It did not take long for the cold and thirsty sailors of the Shenandoah to nose out this tempting item of the cargo, and before the officers knew what was happening, a cask had been broached and the greater part of one watch were hilariously drunk. The inebriated ones were promptly locked into the forecastle, some of the more unruly being placed in irons. But while this was going on, the rest of the crew established contact with the captured treasure, and by the time one detachment was quelled, the others had succeeded in getting themselves in prime condition. Thus, by detachments, the whole crew fell into a gorgeous and monumental spree, and before order was restored there were not a dozen sober men on the ship.

"It seems a shame to burn up all that good liquor," Lieutenant Scales, the boarding officer, wistfully remarked to Captain Waddell as preparations were made for the Abigail's destruction.

"Yes, I believe you're right. Before you touch her off, maybe you'd better bring a little of it aboard— just in case of sickness, you know."

"Aye, aye. About how much shall I bring?"

"Oh, about twenty-five barrels," the captain replied casually, and Mr. Scales went over the side chuckling at the extent of the epidemic of sickness the captain apparently feared.

The captain's little joke, however, put notions into Scales's head. He had been on the sick list himself. Maybe he'd better bring aboard a private keg of that liquor so he'd have an ample supply on which to recuperate. Accordingly he secreted a keg in the room occupied by Blacker, the clerk. Here it was found in the checkup following the outbreak of drunkenness in the crew, and there were prompt and violent repercussions. Scales was summarily suspended. The boatswain's mate, suspected of having a part in the transaction, was broken, disrated. Blacker was banished from the cabin to the steerage.

Blacker was so indiscreet as to attempt to explain his demotion by saying that it was his punishment for refusing to act as the captain's spy on the officers. This reached the ears of Whittle, who reported it to the captain, and Waddell flew into a rage.

"It is an infamous and deliberate falsehood!" he roared, and ordered Blacker called to his cabin. There, with Bulloch and Lining as witnesses, he pilloried the quaking clerk.

"Did I ever ask you to spy on the officers?"

"Well, not exactly, sir, but I rather drew the inference—" Blacker stammered.

"Did I ask you to inform on them?"

"No, sir," Blacker admitted weakly.

"The fact is, gentlemen," said the captain, turning to Lining and Bulloch, "that Mr. Blacker was sent to the steerage for the simple reason that he broke a rule and then lied about it. He said he had no liquor in his room, and later a keg was found there. That is all there is to it."

But although the captain was vindicated in this episode, and although Scales's suspension was almost immediately lifted, the officers continued to view the captain with misgivings. He was not only erratic and vacillating in his judgment; he was a martinet. Confidence in a ship's captain, once lost, is not easily regained, and they were constantly on the alert for faults.

Meantime they whiled away their time with gymnastics and wrestling, exercising with dumb-bells, shooting at sea gulls with their pistols, and interspersing target practice with some lively snowball battles on deck. The days were long, the sun rising at three o'clock and setting at nine, but when other forms of diversion palled, they could always listen to Captain Nye, who was a willing narrator of his wonderful adventures on the high seas during a lifetime of sailing. There was the time when he and six other men were cast adrift in a boat near the Galápagos Islands with only six pieces of hardtack and half a keg of water, but they went 1700 miles in thirteen days and finally landed safely, hungry and thirsty, but alive. Captain Nye was sometimes a bore with his tall tales, but listening to him was better than nursing their own grievances, so they encouraged him in his reminiscing and in the dreary, long arctic twilights drank the seamen's favorite toast, "Sweethearts and wives," in beakers of hot rum punch, and waited for something to turn up.

The Shenandoah cruised slowly on through the Okhotsk, beset by ice on all sides and continually buffeted by the gales which, though generally of only a few hours' duration, were frequent and always violent enough to threaten the vessel's safety. She encountered the first of these furious gales just outside Ghyinsk Bay, to windward of a field of twenty miles of jagged floe ice ranging from fifteen to thirty feet thick, and if she had been hove to with the ice under her lee would probably have been lost with all hands on board. The cruiser was drifting faster than the ice, and it became imperative to find a less hazardous position. Accordingly she was carefully eased along the floe at a little distance from it until the lookout aloft discovered a passage through it with open water beyond. She was then skillfully maneuvered through this passage, and in a short time was snugly lying to under close sail with the floe to windward. In this position the floe not only ceased to be a menace but acted as a breakwater. Calmly and easily the little cruiser now rode in water as smooth as a park lake, while the crashing breakers on the farther edge of the floe threw sheets of spray twenty feet into the air.

The gale was accompanied by a hissing onslaught of sleet and rain which in the subzero weather formed a frosty crust wherever it fell. Soon the braces, blocks, yards, sails, and all running rigging were completely coated in a sheathing of ice from a half inch to two inches thick, so that it was impossible to use the braces. Icicles of enormous size and length hung from all parts of the sails and rigging, and

191

when the sun came out after nine hours of wind and rain, the glittering ship presented a picture of enchantment. From deck to truck she sparkled as if encrusted with diamonds, and the men forgot the discomforts and dangers of the storm as they looked upon the dazzling aftermath.

"She looks just like a ship made of sugar I saw in a candy shop at home once," murmured Mason admiringly.

"It makes me think of a silver ship set with rhinestones I saw in a Cape Town barroom in '59," said the much-traveled Lee.

But there was no time to be wasted in admiring the beauty of the scene. The ice in the rigging was a menace to the safe handling of the vessel. As soon as the storm was over, Captain Waddell sent aloft a detail of men armed with heavy billets of wood to dislodge the ice and free the running gear from its frosty shackles. It was a dangerous task in the treacherous footing afforded by the icy rigging, and as huge chunks of ice came crashing down to the deck there were many narrow escapes from injury.

"This deck cargo of ice would be worth a fortune to us if we had it in Charleston this morning," Grimball remarked.

"Yes, and it's worth a whole lot to us right here and now," the captain agreed. "Remember, that ice is just frozen rainwater. Better put the men to work gathering up enough of it to fill all the empty water tanks and casks."

During the height of the storm the ship had been driven into a floe, and although she was undamaged by the crash, by the time the wind had subsided she was completely blocked in on every side. Therefore, once the rigging had been cleared and the deck freed of its icy sheath, warps and grapnels were run out on the floe and hooked to huge blocks of ice, and under the skillful direction of Lieutenant Lee, the officer of the deck, the ship was gradually worked out of her dangerous position.

As soon as she was in open water again, her course was changed to the eastward. The Shenandoah had never been intended for any such back-breaking service as this, and Captain Waddell, unwilling to subject her unnecessarily to the destructive shock of contact with the grinding Arctic ice, gave up the idea of entering Ghijinsk Bay and stood along the land of Eastern Siberia. The very next evening, despite all precautions, she was jammed in the ice again, and through an anxious night they all lay wide-awake in their bunks, listening to the huge blocks thundering and chafing against the cruiser's side as though bent on her annihilation. None of the officers was experienced in Arctic navigation, and they were not able to judge accurately the imminence of the danger. The hazard seemed greater than it was prudent to risk, however, and after cruising about carefully in the neighborhood of Shantarski Island for another two or three days, without seeing any signs of whalers, Captain Waddell ordered the ship taken out through Amphitrite Strait into the North Pacific. On June 14 she was headed to the northeast, with a cracking southwester behind her, in a course which would take her midway between

Attu, the most western of the Aleutian Islands, and the most eastern of the Komandorski group, and thus into the Bering Sea.

Captain Waddell, poring over his Phillemore, had discovered that it was contrary to the dictates of international maritime law to take an enemy vessel in a river or bay, and so was reconciled to leaving the Okhotsk, where there was not much chance of catching a whaler in the open sea. There had been some talk of standing for St. John Island in the northwestern part of the Okhotsk, but when the captain called a conference of the officers in his cabin they were unanimously opposed to it. Minor, who was supposed to know something about whaling and the habits of the whalers, said positively that the ice made it impossible to get to St. John, and so there seemed no course left but to move on into the Bering.

During all this time, although seeing no whalers, they saw plenty of whales. The giant mammals, swimming boldly about the cruiser's sides, were a novel sight to most of the officers and crew, who watched their antics with eager interest. The unfortunate Chew, in fact, became so engrossed in the sight that he leaned too far over the rail and thus dropped his last and only uniform cap, but when a boat was lowered, he succeeded in rescuing it.

Before leaving the Okhotsk, poor Canning, still suffering from the unhealed wound he had received at Shiloh, asked Dr. Lining to request the captain to set him ashore on the Siberian coast. Once ashore, he said, he could make his way to the Amor River and thence to Europe, where he could seek hospitalization.

"I'll never get well aboard this ship," he said to Lining with sad prescience. The doctor secretly agreed with him and promised to relay his request to the captain. Waddell, however, saw that it would be foolhardy for a sick man to try to travel half way around the world from the snowy coast of Siberia and refused to entertain the idea.

Within a few hours after the Shenandoah left the Okhotsk, the sea was enveloped in an impenetrable, thick, black fog which shut down on the vessel like a candle-snuffer. But Captain Waddell pressed on. For forty-eight hours, with his heart in his throat, he laid the course by dead reckoning, without benefit of observation, and it was not until the evening of the second day that the wind shifted and as though by an act of Providence the damp, fleecy blanket lifted sufficiently for the lookout to get a view of the course ahead. It was not a minute too soon either. Hardly had the mists parted when the cry of "Land ho!" rang out, and ghost-like on the port bow there loomed a shadowy headland.

"Copper Island!" exclaimed Grimball, the officer of the deck, then hastily gave the orders to change the course. With groaning timbers and flapping canvas the little cruiser veered about and avoided shipwreck. Then, almost as suddenly as it had lifted, the fog descended again, and once more they were enveloped in its muffling pall. At the same time the wind died down to a dead calm, but Waddell furled sails, ordered steam up, and groped into the Bering Sea on the afternoon of June 16.

It was a desperately dangerous business, threading those unfamiliar channels in the northern seas, but at the very time when it was most needed, help came suddenly from the least expected source. The second mate of the Abigail, Thomas L. Manning, appeared before the captain one morning and without mincing words announced his desire to join the Shenandoah's crew.

"What you need up here," he said, and Captain Waddell knew he spoke the truth, "is a pilot. These waters around the Aleutians are famous for fogs, especially in the summer time. You might possibly be lucky enough to get through here by the help of your charts, and again you might not. Now me, I'm a pilot. I know these seas like you know the deck of your ship. You need me, and I'd be satisfied with a petty officer's commission. I was born in Baltimore, and down in my heart I'm a Southern sympathizer. So if you want a pilot, I'm your man."

Captain Waddell in his extremity did not hesitate. He was keenly aware of the dangers incident to blundering about in unfamiliar seas, choked with ice and shrouded in fogs, and he gladly welcomed the new addition to his force. So Manning, after being duly enrolled as a ship's corporal and issued a Confederate uniform, entered upon his duties with as much enthusiasm as though he had been one of the original crew. Having entered the service, he did nothing by halves but set actively to work trying to induce as many as possible of his shipmates to follow his example, and several of them did so. On the other hand, a number of the Abigail's crew were loud and blunt in their denunciation of him.

"A Southerner he is now, is he?" said one of them contemptuously. "Ask him about how he voted for Abe Lincoln in San Francisco just before he shipped with us—sold his vote for a drink of rotgut whiskey. He was saying then that he was born in Boston."

The cruiser's officers largely shared his mates' contempt for the turncoat, but he was a good pilot, so they swallowed their feelings and accepted his services.

With Manning at the wheel and with the favor of a fair wind they now made good sailing, and after a favorable passage of nine days they sighted and stood toward Cape Thaddeus on the coast of Siberia. This cape is located exactly on the 180th meridian, opposite Greenwich, and is frequented by whalers for the purpose of regulating their chronometers. The cape was deserted when sighted on June 21, but the next day, in a northeast current, blubber was seen floating on the water, which Manning greeted with a shout.

"That's a sure sign of whalers," the pilot announced. "There's cutting out going on southwest of here."

At his suggestion the cruiser was turned in that direction. Manning's calculation was well founded, for within less than an hour the lookout at the masthead shouted that he had sighted two sails dead ahead.

Soon the cruiser came up with the William Thompson and the Euphrates, both of New Bedford, the Thompson having the distinction of being the largest whaler out of New England. Hardly had prize crews been placed aboard when another sail was seen, and the Shenandoah set out after her, showing the Russian flag. It proved to be a British whaling vessel, the Robert L. Townes of Sydney. Her master hailed the Shenandoah sharply.

"What ship is that?"

"The Petropawlowka," Captain Waddell gravely replied, still maintaining the guise of a Russian, and steamed back to put the torch to the William Thompson and the Euphrates.

The following day, again marked June 22, as the 180th meridian had been passed during the night, five vessels were sighted near a large body of floe ice. The nearest two were found to be neutrals, but the Shenandoah, flying the American flag, ran close to the stern of the next one, the Milo of New Bedford, and Captain Howe was ordered to come aboard with his papers. He was a very much surprised captain when he learned the identity of the steamer. He had heard of her being in Australia, but had hardly expected to encounter her in the Bering Sea.

"But what are you doing up here now, anyhow? Don't you know the war's over?"

"The war's over?" repeated Waddell incredulously. "Don't try any of your Yankee tricks on me. I'll not be fooled so easily. What makes you think it's over? Who says so? Have you got any proof?"

"Well," the whaler's captain qualified, "I believe it's over from what I heard in Frisco in April. They were saying there that Lee had surrendered and the South was whipped."

"Just a Yankee trick," repeated Waddell, unwilling to believe the news. "I know Lee hasn't surrendered, and, even if he has, that doesn't mean the war's over, does it? Unless you've got more proof than just some loose waterfront gossip, you'll have to submit to capture."

Shrugging his shoulders, Captain Howe admitted that he had no documentary proof, and was preparing to submit to the destruction of the Milo when Captain Waddell offered to spare his vessel if he would give bond and receive on board all the prisoners the cruiser wanted to send back. Howe eagerly consented to this arrangement and at Waddell's direction sent his crew in their boats to the cruiser to receive the prisoners he was to carry back to the States.

With the Milo's crew taken temporarily on board, thus leaving that vessel helpless even if she wanted to try to escape, the Shenandoah then set off in pursuit of the two nearest whalers, who seemed to be concocting a plan of escape. Both of them were frantically heading for the field ice, evidently believing that while the cruiser was chasing one, the other might find some opening through which she could escape. The Shenandoah got up steam and briskly stood after them. As she approached within easy range, one put about and steered for the shore, while the other stood on into the ice. With the lookout keeping a sharp eye on the former, they gave their immediate attention to one nearing the ice. They fired a solid shot that passed just forward of her figurehead. Still she pushed on through the ice in the desperate hope of escaping, so another shot was fired, this one tearing through her main topsail. This served to convince the fugitive that escape was impossible, so she submitted and was speedily boarded by the prize crew commanded by Lieutenant Scales. It was the Sophia Thornton of New Bedford. As soon as the cruiser's men had taken charge of her, the Shenandoah started in pursuit of the other whaler, under steam and fore-and-aft sail.

After a lively chase of three hours she was overhauled and brought to with a shot from the thirty-two pound Whitworth rifle, although she had crowded on all sail in her effort to make a dash for the safety afforded if she could get within a league of the Siberian coast. It was the Jireh Swift, an appropriately named fast bark, under Captain Williams, and although the captain made a plucky and obstinate effort to save his bark, he saw the folly of exposing her crew to a warship's destructive fire when he was overhauled. He yielded to his misfortune with becoming and manly dignity. When Lieutenant Lee boarded the bark he found the Captain with his gripsack packed and the men stuffing their effects into their ditty bags. Within twenty minutes the Jireh Swift was in flames.

Captain Williams talked freely about the war, and advanced the opinion that the South had made a mistake in not sending a cruiser to the Arctic regions two years before.

"This is the kind of thing that really hurts," he said frankly. "Why, one of these barks, with her oil and bone, is worth a quarter of a million or more, and when they find out in New Bedford that you're sinking them by the dozen it will stir them up more than ten battles in Virginia."

He seemed not averse to discussing matters in a spirit of frankness, so Captain Waddell asked him pointedly, "Do you believe the war is over?"

"No, I don't believe it's over, but I do believe that the South will have to yield sooner or later. What you're doing up here now is useless. It's too late. But two years ago you might have brought New England to her knees by a raid like this."

But Captain Waddell had no time to discuss politics. The prisoners were loaded, bag and baggage, into the Milo, which had been plentifully supplied with stores from the Thornton, and after giving Captain Howe a certificate stating why he was without his register, Waddell sent the ship off to San Francisco. The captain then turned to Whittle.

"It will give Secretary Mallory a thrill in Richmond when he gets the news of our whereabouts and the success of our activities. And I know it will please President Davis."

CHAPTER FIFTEEN

WHOLESALE DESTRUCTION

THE SHENANDOAH was now fairly in the land of the midnight sun, operating in a day of six months' duration. In the subzero weather, with snow falling nearly every day, and constantly menaced by ice floes and towering icebergs, it was at least some consolation to have the boon of constant daylight. The sun was in its highest northern declination, and even when it dipped for a few minutes each night beneath the northern horizon, a bright golden fringe marked its course until its pale and cheerless face rose again over iceberg and snow.

So far the cruiser had been running under steam, but coal was too precious to be wasted unless absolutely necessary. Now, under sail and with fires banked, she stood to the northward, making for the Arctic Ocean and the whalers supposed to be congregated there.

Soon after passing St. Lawrence Island there was a pleasant diversion from the serious business in hand when the cruiser was visited by a little fleet of native canoes, manned by jabbering Eskimos, who wanted to trade furs and walrus tusks for whiskey and tobacco or whatever trinkets the sailors might have to spare. To most of the crew and to all of the officers this was a novel and interesting experience. Even Captain Waddell, for all his long experience in the Navy, had never before penetrated Arctic waters nor had contact with the Eskimos. He ordered the Shenandoah hove to while the men excitedly talked and traded with the swarthy natives. When at length they parted company, the cruiser's officers and men were loaded down with walrus ivory souvenirs and seal-skins, and the Eskimos had a year's supply of to-bacco and red liquor.

Late the next day, the twenty-third, a sail was over-hauled, the brig Susan Abigail, of San Francisco. The Susan Abigail, however, was no whaler. She was a trading vessel loaded with a miscellaneous cargo of cheap guns, pistols, needles, calico, twine, and other Yankee notions, all of which had a high trading value with the natives whose only wealth was measured in furs and sealskins and walrus tusks. It was a highly remunerative business for the traders. An old musket and some ammunition could be ex-changed for fifteen or twenty sables, and a good knife would purchase almost anything an Eskimo possessed.

The captain of the Susan Abigail was more a business man than a sailor. When he came on board the cruiser, he was richly attired in a splendid fur coat and sealskin cap, relics of his last voyage to the Arctic seas, and he looked the successful, opulent trader that he was. Indeed, he promptly volunteered the statement that he had grown wealthy in the trade, that he had planned for this to be his last trip, that he had expected to clear at least $30,000 on this voyage, and then retire from business. On the basis of this novel and nebulous claim to immunity he suggested that his ship ought to be spared from destruction, and pressed this idea very earnestly. But all his eloquence failed to impress Captain Waddell.

Waddell was impressed, however, by something he found on board the brig—California newspapers containing the latest despatches from the war. Lee had indeed surrendered, incredible as such news was to the loyal Captain Waddell. Richmond had been evacuated, and President Davis and his cabinet had fled to Danville. But, it was also stated, part of Lee's army had escaped and joined General Johnston in North Carolina, where they had just given battle to General Sherman, and there was a proclamation issued by President Davis announcing that, despite the reverses, the war would be carried on with renewed vigor, exhorting the Southern people to bear up heroically and continue the struggle.

Captain Waddell was shaken by the news, although gratified to find that, at least so far as these papers stated, the war was not yet actually at an end. Soberly he pondered his duty in view of the President's proclamation of continued resistance.

"What is the opinion about the war in San Francisco," he asked. "How long do they think it will last?"

The captain said frankly that opinion was divided in California.

"It looks very plain to me that the North has the

better of it right now. With Lee surrendered, there's no denying they have the advantage. But you never can tell. Nobody can know for certain how it will end or how long it will last. And of course," he added with a snort, "you can't place any dependence in the newspapers. Half the stuff they print is just a pack of lies."

The captain's uncertainty about the outcome of the war seemed to be shared by his crew. At any rate, without solicitation three of these adventurous spirits volunteered to join on the Shenandoah, attracted by the prospect of adventure and apparently not being bound by strong ties of loyalty to any particular flag, and they were accordingly added to Lieutenant Whittle's budding marine corps.

With the California papers before them, Captain Waddell discussed the matter informally with his officers. The affairs of the Confederacy, it was plain to even the most reluctant disbeliever, had just about reached the stage of a forlorn hope. But President Davis was still maintaining resistance and urging the people of the South to do likewise. What should the Shenandoah do? As long as any shadow of the Confederate government existed, could she properly entertain any idea of abandoning her efforts just because of reverses suffered by the armies in the field? Could she, in fact, honorably do otherwise than continue about her appointed duties so long as there appeared to be a vestige of hope? Waddell presented the case to them and invited their views. They were unanimously of one opinion. They must go ahead.

"Thank you, gentlemen," the Captain pronounced quietly. "We shall proceed with the cruise."

On the twenty-fifth, faced by a field of ice stretching as far as sight could reach, the cruiser resumed steaming again, and to avoid the ice stood directly north.

During the morning two vessels were sighted, but they were both neutrals, an Hawaiian and a Frenchman. In the afternoon of the same day the Shenandoah came up with the General Williams, of New Bedford, which promptly surrendered when the cruiser showed the Confederate flag.

The Captain of the General Williams proved to be a bad loser. He took his capture very much to heart, and as he came over the side with his papers, he began to bluster.

"What is the meaning of this? What have I ever done to you that you should hunt me down like a wild animal and destroy my property? Have I ever done you any injury?"

"There is nothing personal about it, I assure you," Whittle replied. "Our blows are aimed at your government. We're in a war, you know."

"That's no excuse! You've got no right to burn my ship. I never did anything to you." And he refused to be comforted.

"I do believe," Scales remarked facetiously, to Whittle, "that that old shellback thinks the Shenandoah came up here in the Arctic Ocean especially to look for the General Williams just out of spite. Listen to him still whining to the skipper."

But, despite his agonized protests, his ship was set afire, and, almost as painful to him, his $400 ship's money was added to the prize fund in the cruiser's iron safe.

Up to this time the Shenandoah had been glad to find her victims singly, or at best, in groups of two or three per day. But on the twenty-sixth she flushed a veritable covey of six whalers, valued with their contents at close to half a million dollars. All of them were destroyed with the exception of one which was ransomed to take the accumulated prisoners back to America.

The first three encountered were the William C. Nye, the Nimrod, and the Catherine, all of New Bedford. As the sea was dead calm, no difficulty was experienced in capturing them. Already the cruiser had on board more than one hundred prisoners, more than it could comfortably and safely accommodate. Since the new accessions would bring the number up to more than 250, it was considered hazardous to have that many hostile passengers aboard the vessel. Other prospective victims were in sight, one of which could be ransomed, but temporarily the newest lot of prisoners were placed for safekeeping in twelve whaleboats and taken in tow by the cruiser. Leaving behind the three blazing ships, wildly drifting amid the glittering icebergs, with the long string of whaleboats following like a kite tail, the Shenandoah stood for the other whalers, now evidently aware of their danger but unable to do anything about it. The cruiser could make barely six knots through the treacherous field of ice, so intricate was the navigation and so careful must she be of the prisoners' boats bobbing like corks in her wake. At length, however, she safely reached the vessels.

Warned that one of the whalers had smallpox on board, Waddell carefully gave her a wide berth and turned his attention to the nearest, the General Pike of New Bedford. The master of the General Pike turned out to be a shrewd and clever young business man. As soon as he was brought before Waddell he took the initiative.

"They tell me you've got to ransom somebody to take your prisoners back to the States," he began. "Now it makes no difference to you whether you ransom my ship or one of the others, but it makes a big difference to me. I shipped out as first mate, and I'm now in command only because the captain has died since we left New Bedford. If I lose my ship, though it's no fault of mine, it can't help giving me a sort of a black eye with the owners. But if I can take her back, even under bond, they are bound to appreciate my getting her back out of this scrape and it will give me a claim on them for the command. What do you say?"

Amused and pleased with the young man's enterprise, Captain Waddell agreed to bond the General Pike, and as arrangements were being made to transfer the prisoners aboard her, a party was sent to take charge of the next victim, the Gipsey.

The captain of the Gipsey was of different mold from the bold master of the Pike. He met the boarding party at the rail, pale and trembling, and obviously frightened out of his wits.

"Spare me!" he pleaded as soon as the Confederates stepped on his deck. "Burn my vessel if you have to, but don't take my life, I beg you!"

He had apparently accepted at full face value all the yarns he had heard and read in the newspapers about the blood-thirsty Rebel pirates, and it was with difficulty that he was at last convinced that he would not be strung up to a yardarm or left aboard his vessel to be burned alive with her. He could scarcely believe it when told that he was to gather up his personal effects and go aboard the General Pike to be returned to San Francisco.

Examination of the Gipsey disclosed that the captain cruised in style. His cabin was most luxuriously fitted up with a beautiful mahogany desk, with other furniture suited to a well-appointed drawing room, and boasted a library of two hundred volumes. He also had a well-stocked wine cellar, and when finally convinced that his life was to be spared, he pressed upon the boarding crew several bottles of his choicest vintages in token of his appreciation of their mercy.

The Isabella, also of New Bedford, was the next and last prize of that busy day. The cruiser was brought alongside to fill her tanks from the Isabella's water casks. Then the Isabella was set on fire, and the cruiser steamed away.

"Not a bad day!" Captain Waddell remarked that night with a glow of satisfaction, and Lieutenant Whittle was bound to confess that it was a very good day indeed.

The next morning, the twenty-seventh, still standing to the northward, the cruiser came upon eleven enemy whalers, plainly in view, placidly tacking about, little suspecting how imminently danger was hanging over them. But the Captain found it necessary to act with caution and deception if he was to carry off this exploit. A stiff breeze was blowing, and if the cruiser showed her colors at once, it was inevitable that some of the prospective victims would be able to make sail and escape in the confusion.

"We must wait for a calm," said Waddell. "Then we shall be able to bag them all. And a fleet like that is worth waiting a day or two for. We needn't be in a hurry."

Accordingly the fires were banked, the telescopic smokestack was lowered, and the wolf in the fold, striving to maintain an innocent appearance, continued in the rear of the whalers, keeping a luff and trying to retard her progress as much as possible. Fortunately for the raider's plans, the next morning a dead calm ensued, the whalers' sails flapped helplessly. Then the cruiser raised her funnel, got up steam, and, flying the American flag, steamed in among the unsuspecting fleet of idle ships.

Before throwing off her disguise, however, the Shenandoah began to make ready for the kill. Five boarding crews, one for each of her available boats, were detailed, and orders were given to board and capture five of the whalers simultaneously. While these preparations were going on, a small boat came off from one of the whalers, the Brunswick, and innocently pulled for the cruiser. Upon closer scrutiny it was seen that the Brunswick had a decided list. When the visiting petty officer came on board, still suspicious of no danger, he explained that she had been stove in by the ice and that his captain wanted to ask for the help of a carpenter to repair her side.

"We are mighty busy right now," Lieutenant Grimball told him courteously, restraining a temptation to smile at the Yankee's impending surprise. "But we'll attend to the Brunswick in just a few minutes. Just be patient and we'll fix you so you won't have to worry any more about that stove-in side."

When the boarding crews were ready, the five boats made off at once for the five nearest whalers, and at the same time the Confederate flag went fluttering up to the cruiser's masthead. On every whaler's deck anxious groups first gazed closely at the perfidious stranger who had stolen into their midst and then looked wistfully aloft at their idle sails hanging useless in the still air.

But there was one notable exception to the general air of helplessness and dejection. Ten of the whalers promptly lowered their flags when the Confederate colors were shown, but the doughty old captain of the Favorite was made of sterner stuff. As soon as he saw the danger threatening, he mustered his men on deck, armed them with muskets, got up the bomb gun used to discharge the harpoon into whales, and stood resolutely on the defensive, a cutlass in one hand and a navy revolver in the other, his flag still flying defiantly.

"Boat ahoy!" he bellowed belligerently at the

boarding crew as soon as they came within hailing distance.

"Ahoy," replied Bulloch, the officer in charge, unaccustomed to such a show of resistance and somewhat abashed at it.

"Who are you and what do you want?"

"We come to inform you that your vessel is a prize to the Confederate States cruiser Shenandoah."

"I'll be damned if she is," hurled back the defiant Yankee. "Not yet. Keep off, I warn you, or I'll fire into you."

With that he began to take sight with his formidable-looking bomb gun. The men cocked their muskets in a businesslike manner, and it was obvious that here was one vessel which was not to be boarded without trouble.

Seeing this, Lieutenant Bulloch rowed back to the cruiser and inquired if it was the captain's desire that he should board her in spite of resistance.

"If I'm any judge," he told Captain Waddell, "the skipper's courage is largely Dutch. He's so drunk he can hardly stand up."

"Well, we'll see if we can't persuade him," Captain Waddell said, and ordered the men back aboard the Shenandoah, which then steamed toward the defiant whaler and stood alongside. The pugnacious skipper still stood resolutely though unsteadily by his bomb gun, and gave every indication of a determination to fight it out in spite of the disparity in strength.

"Haul down your flag!" thundered Lieutenant Chew, the officer of the deck, in his sternest tone of voice.

"Haul it down yourself, God damn you, if you think it will be good for your constitution."

"Don't be a fool," counseled Chew. "If you don't haul down your flag, we'll blow you out of the water in five minutes."

"Blow away, my buck," returned the still unsubdued captain. "I'll be eternally damned if I haul down that flag for any Rebel pirate that ever floated."

"Very well," replied Mr. Chew. Turning to the gunner he said in a loud tone, "Load the starboard Whitworth, and when you fire let her have it in the hull right at the water-line. This foolishness has gone far enough."

"Now," he continued to the whaler's crew, "if every person isn't off that tub in five minutes, down she goes. Stand ready, Mr. Guy."

The crew of the Favorite came off in their boats before the five minutes were up, but the captain stood swaying by the rail, still howling his profane defiance.

Captain Waddell had stood an amused spectator to this unwonted scene, and so much did he admire the old fellow's spirit that he would not permit a shot to be fired. Instead he dispatched another armed boat's crew, this time under the diplomatic Lieutenant Whittle, to bring him off. Whittle lived up to his reputation as a persuasive and convincing talker and orally overpowered the unwilling captive, convincing him of the folly of singlehandedly defying a warship, and induced him to submit peaceably. As he finally clambered down into the small boat, still mumbling incoherent imprecations, it was obvious to all that he was in the last stages of inebriation. But he was given a cheer as he came over the cruiser's rail, and by general consent of the Shenandoah's crew was deemed the bravest and most resolute man they had encountered during their cruise.

One by one the other whalers were boarded and prepared for destruction, a work which by this time had become a routine and humdrum affair for the Shenandoah's men.

One of the prizes proved to be the James Maury, a vessel for which Captain Waddell was particularly on the lookout. He had heard her tragic story from the whalers at Ponape and had learned after reaching the Arctic that she was somewhere in those waters. The unfortunate captain-owner of this vessel had died during the early stages of his voyage, and to add to the tragedy of the death he had with him on board his young wife and two small children. To avoid the dismal burial at sea, the Spartan widow had ordered his body preserved in a cask of whisky, to be returned for burial in the soil of his native New England. She and her children had continued on the voyage, heroically refusing the acting master's suggestion that they turn back. Captain Waddell sent Chew aboard to assure her that no harm would come to her and her children.

"Tell her," he instructed, "that on her account the James Maury will be spared and that she will be permitted to go back to New Bedford with her children carrying her husband's body with her."

The poor widow had been viewing with growing

apprehension the capture of the other whalers, and was almost in a state of collapse from fright when Lieutenant Chew stepped on board the Maury. Immediately and earnestly she besought him, with tears in her eyes, not to destroy the ship which had been her husband's home for so long. As gently as possible he soothed her fears, telling her of Captain Waddell's specific instructions that no harm should befall her or the ship which was now her property and means of livelihood. When she realized that she was to be spared the fate of the other members of the fleet, her apprehension quickly turned to effusive and tearful gratitude.

No mercy was shown any of the others, however, except that the Nile was ransomed to be used, in conjunction with the James Maury, in taking more than three hundred prisoners back to the States.

Not all the prisoners, it developed, wanted to go back. Nine of them joined the crew of the Shenandoah, some of them veterans of the Union army, and these Whittle gladly added to his little marine corps.

Aside from the James Maury and the Nile, the haul for the day was five barks, the Waverly, Martha, Favorite, Covington, and Congress; and four ships, the Hillman, Nassau, Brunswick, and Isaac Howland.

A little surprise party was held on the Shenandoah's deck when Captain Manning of the Hillman came on board and saw the pilot at the wheel.

"My God!" he exclaimed. "My brother! We're both victims of this damned pirate!" But he was

215

aghast with amazement and indignation when he realized that his brother was present on the Rebel cruiser as a member of the crew and not as a prisoner.

"Why, you—you—" the master of the Hillman sputtered. "You're a traitor to your flag. You're a disgrace to the Manning family. Why, I'd rather see you dead and in hell than in that damned gray uniform. I'll never be able to hold my head up in New Bedford again."

"Take it easy, take it easy," soothed the pilot. "It's just a business matter with me. I'm on the ship's papers, drawing down my pay. Ain't that better than being in the brig? And ain't it better than being set down in San Francisco without a ship under your feet, like you'll be? Why don't you join up with us yourself? Maybe I could get the skipper to make a place for you. Think it over."

But the elder Manning was not to be proselytized, and when he went aboard the Nile with his luggage, he was still shaking his head in shame at the thought of his brother in a Rebel uniform.

That night the Arctic was lighted up with the greatest conflagration ever seen in those northern seas. The brilliance of the Aurora Borealis itself was rivaled as the nine whalers, with all their inflammable contents, sent up a red glare which was reflected for miles in the drifting, glistening ice, and the roaring and crackling of the flames made weird music to the ship's company on the Shenandoah as they stood away at a safe distance and watched the climax of the day's destruction.

In the distance the Nile and the James Maury were slowly pushing through the floes on their way back to civilization, and Captain Waddell looked in that direction as much as he looked at the whalers' bonfire.

"Another great day for the cause, Mr. Whittle. A great day for the Confederacy—but I keep thinking of that poor widow. I hope she gets back safely. War is a cruel thing, Mr. Whittle. I wish we were out of it."

Waddell did not know it then. He was, as a matter of fact, already out of it. That day he had struck the last armed blow that was struck for the Confederacy. The blazing whalers constituted a funeral pyre for the Lost Cause. The war was over. The last hostile gesture had been made. The Shenandoah's work was finished.

CHAPTER SIXTEEN

LEAVING THE ARCTIC

W HILE THE NINE WHALERS were still blazing in
the twilight of the Arctic midnight, the Shenandoah hove up her kedge and once again resumed
her northward route. Slowly pushing her way on
through the drifting floes she passed through the
Bering Straits, with the outpost capes of Asia and
North America in sight to port and starboard.

Once fairly out on the forbidding Arctic Ocean,
the cruiser met a formidable prospect. Leaving the
capes far behind her, for hour after hour she steamed
on into the frozen solitude. As far as the eye could
reach, to every horizon, there stretched only mounting fields of sawtooth ice. Not a sail was sighted after
leaving the burning whalers. While the steamer
ground her way slowly through the crunching ice,
grave doubts began to enter Captain Waddell's mind
as to whether he could expect to find any more of the
New England fleet to the northward. Pilot Manning
professed to believe that there were more whalers up
there somewhere, but as time passed and the lookouts'
glasses still revealed nothing on the horizon but ice

and still more ice, the captain's doubts increased.

Every day the ice was growing thicker, and the size of the bergs was mounting. The season of open water was fast slipping away, and there was imminent danger that the little cruiser, unprepared for any such ordeal, might be trapped in the Arctic wastes until the coming of open weather again next year. After all, the Captain reasoned, his first duty was to save his ship from destruction and preserve her usefulness. There was nothing to be gained by a bullheaded persistence in plunging ahead in those murderous ice fields in the faint hope of finding more victims, especially when there was always the danger of being caught in the ice. The Shenandoah was not built for such strenuous service; to be frozen in there would inevitably mean destruction of the ship and probably the loss of all on board.

At last, therefore, Captain Waddell reluctantly gave the order to turn the prow southward, and he had the satisfaction of reaching East Cape just in time to slip by the Diomedes before a vast field of floe ice closed the strait. Even then the ship was forced to fight her way through, but she shoved forward slowly. Every kind of precaution was observed to save her from injury. Strong rope mats were hung over her cutwater and bows to give protection against the saw-like edges of the jagged ice. Carefully, through shifting fogs, she steamed southward, her shivering men dreaming of the tropic seas they soon were to see again.

"It is well you decided to leave the Arctic when

you did, sir," Whittle remarked to the Captain when they had made the passage. "Another day might have been too late. That ice is closing in fast."

"Yes, it was a narrow squeak," agreed Waddell. "I don't believe I would have enjoyed being frozen in for the winter. I'm willing to leave that to the Polar explorers."

When the island of St. Lawrence was passed on the outward trip, there was a fine wind from the northwest, and Waddell, ever frugal with his precious supply of coal, triced up the propeller and ordered sail to be made again. Hardly had the change been made when one of the recurring dense fogs settled down and so obscured the view that before Lieutenant Lee, the officer of the deck, had time to shorten sail he found her in pilot ice, ever the danger sign in those waters. While the Shenandoah was still under way, a giant berg suddenly thrust its towering bulk through the enveloping fog. With a terrifying impact the cruised rammed her bow into the mountain of ice. Officers and men were thrown from their berths and hammocks, and for a time, in the confusion, the impression prevailed that she had struck a rock and would probably go down. The force of the collision was so great that she was thrown backward suddenly and heavily. She immediately gathered sternboard, which threw her against the ice in the rear with another crashing impact. Lieutenant Lee acted rapidly and speedily, despite the confusion and the unexpectedness of the emergency. Amid the hubbub on board, with the officers' shouts muffled by close-hanging fog, all sail was speedily reefed. Her backward progress was effectually stopped by the ice jam behind her. So there she was, closely bottled in with ice on all sides from twenty to thirty feet thick—a dangerous prospect indeed for a merchant ship designed for the ordinary navigation of the open seas.

But Captain Waddell was not dismayed by his predicament. He immediately sent a number of the crew over the side onto the floe, where they made lines fast by means of crowbars and kedges secured in the ice. Her head was gradually warped around to the desired direction. With rope mats protecting her bows and a low head of steam, her cutwater pushed a large block of ice like a giant wedge, opening a track through which, after a struggle lasting for seven hours, she emerged into open water.

"Thank God!" murmured Captain Waddell, and that earnest exclamation was re-echoed throughout the ship from wardroom to forecastle as the fog slowly lifted and the menacing ice was left behind.

The Shenandoah was still fairly within the usual whaling ground, and the Captain was reluctant to leave the region if it were possible to take more prizes, but his hopes gradually withered as day after day passed without sighting another vessel. He called Lieutenant Whittle into his cabin.

"I am inclined to believe, Mr. Whittle," he said, "that the time has come for us to take the steamer out of these waters into more open seas. By this time I think our presence here must certainly be known to some of the enemy's cruisers on the Pacific or China station. We have sent several cartels back, neutral vessels have sighted us, and there have been the burning ships to give warning. Knowing that we are here, it would not be difficult for them to blockade us in the Bering Sea or, possibly, to force us into action."

"I would fear a blockade in the ice," Whittle agreed. "We might not be able to stand that. But unless they outnumber us too heavily, I'd rather welcome some action. I believe we could hold our own."

"That does credit to your courage," the Captain said smilingly, "but, I fear, not to your judgment. It would not be sensible or good policy for us to risk the cruiser in a contest which would put us in need of repairs in port, even if we won. Where could we turn for repairs today? There is only one wise course."

"And what is that?" Whittle asked respectfully.

"We've done all the harm we can to the whalers. My idea now is to steam down off the coast of Lower California and Mexico and lie in wait for the steamers plying between Panama and California. We might pick up some rich prizes there, and certainly we can do nothing further up here."

Whittle was forced to agree with the logic of this reasoning, and he immediately told the other officers of the new plan. There was still one obstacle to be overcome, however, before this plan could be followed. Having got into the Bering Sea through the encircling chain of the Aleutian islands several weeks before, it was now necessary to get out again. For days a typically dense, black Aleutian fog had enveloped everything, shutting out a view of the sky and of all objects fifty yards distant. Still the steamer pressed on through the murk in the direction of Amukta Pass, that passage in the Aleutians on the 172nd meridian. The enveloping mists rendered the navigation instruments largely useless, but Captain Waddell closely watched his charts and his compass and boldly proceeded by dead reckoning, aiming for the center of the passage and hoping for the best. When his calculations indicated that the pass was near at hand, the fog still continued thick and gloomy and all-obscuring. But the cruiser dashed along on her course, the Captain trusting to the accuracy of his calculations and a fervent hope that the fog might lift so that land might be sighted in time should she fail to strike open water.

Nerves tingling, like a blind man groping his way through a dark room, Captain Waddell paced the quarter-deck and peered into the deep gloom encompassing him. It seemed foolhardy to steam blindly ahead, but it would have been a culpable error to stop steaming or to attempt to run in a circle until the fog should lift. In a sea and near islands where currents are irregular in direction and force, the drift of a ship might easily prove more dangerous than running on a direct course from last observations. Steaming ahead, dangerous as it was, was the safest thing he could do.

When Waddell calculated that the ship should be about at the center of the pass, he was overjoyed when the fog began to lift and his straining eyes could dimly discern land off either beam. Like a

marksman shooting in the dark, he had hit the bulls-
eye, and as the dull blur of the land on either side
was seen faintly through the thinning mist, a great
load of anxiety rolled off his shoulders.

"We are headed for the open Pacific now, Mr.
Whittle," he breathed to the chief officer. "The ship
is safe now. I believe I'll go below."

CHAPTER SEVENTEEN

THE SAD NEWS

O N THE FOURTH OF JULY the Shenandoah, feeling her way through the soupy fog, slipped
through the chain of the Aleutians which threatened
to imprison her in the frozen Bering Sea and steamed
out into the North Pacific to transfer her destructive
activities from the whaling fleet to the rich merchant
ships plying the Californian coast.

Throughout the North people were celebrating
this first recurrence of the national holiday since
their victory of the preceding April. In the South
the people were settling down to the dreary task of
rebuilding their shattered lives. The government of
the Confederate States of America was now but a
memory. Its president and vice-president were in
prison. Its cabinet members were scattered to the
corners of the earth. The Confederate Navy Department no longer existed. Its records had been captured or destroyed, and Secretary Mallory was now
just a private citizen out of a job wondering whether
he would be arrested for treason.

Out there in the North Pacific, its government
crumbled into nothing, its flag representing no living

authority, the Shenandoah was now nothing but an outlaw, albeit an innocent outlaw, and all but forgotten by those who had placed their dependence in her.

She was not quite forgotten, however. Far off in England the faithful Bulloch still maintained a firm appreciation of his responsibilities, despite the failure of his government. By June 1 it had been finally though regretfully impressed on him, through the slow process of transatlantic correspondence, that the Southern Confederacy had ceased to exist. In the shock of that fateful news, one of his very first thoughts had been of the plight of the Shenandoah, out on the high seas he did not know where, still ignorant of the untoward turn of affairs back home. He had sent the Shenandoah out; he must do all that he could to get her back safely.

Promptly Bulloch communicated with Mason, the Confederate commissioner in England, and between them they composed a letter of instructions to be forwarded to Captain Waddell in whatever way might be found possible, officially advising him of the end of the war and instructing him to disarm his cruiser and make his way to England. Mason then sought the assistance of Earl Russell, the British secretary for foreign affairs, submitting the proposed letter of instructions and asking that the British government co-operate by sending it to its consuls at Nagasaki, Shanghai, and the Sandwich Islands, in the hope that they might find an opportunity to transmit it to the commander of the wandering cruiser. His Lordship consented to send the letter to the points suggested, and also volunteered to send a copy of it to all British colonial authorities, for the purpose of reaching the Shenandoah wherever she might happen to touch. Passage through the red tape of the British foreign office, however, took time, and it was July 12 before the letter actually went out in the mails from Downing Street.

Meanwhile the Shenandoah was jogging along with light air, occasionally running before a gale, until she reached the meridian of 129°. There she took the north wind which sweeps down the California coast and followed a course roughly parallel with the land, though several hundred miles out from it. A sharp lookout was maintained aloft, for she was now in waters frequented by the United States warships, and in these circumstances the cruiser was playing the double role of hunter and hunted.

Despite the increased hazards, however, a general feeling of confidence and cheerfulness pervaded the officers and crew. She had done her work well in the northern waters. She had accomplished her mission, and she had come safely through all the perils of those unfamiliar and unfriendly seas. The ice and snow were just a memory now. Pea jackets and woolen underwear had gone back into the chests, and a watch on deck had now become a pleasant pastime instead of a dangerous and irksome duty. The crew were putting in their time cleaning and painting the ship, and within a few days the battered and weather-beaten look she had acquired while boxing about in the Arctic ice had disappeared, and she once more assumed her oldtime tidiness.

The officers now had little to do, and the rage for chess and whist burst out again. There was also more recourse to the cruiser's scanty library. Dr. Lining took up the study of Maury's *Physical Geography of the Sea* and began to keep a daily thermometer and hydrometer record to be turned over to Maury later. Lining was handicapped by the fact that he had no hydrometer, but he ingeniously used his urinometer for this purpose.

"Maury will know how to make the necessary corrections," he told Whittle, to whom he confided his record-keeping plans.

A pleasant event during this stage of the cruise was the celebration on July 13 of Captain Waddell's forty-first birthday. Both the captain and the officers were thoroughly cognizant of the widening gulf between them, but the officers were strong on the amenities, and on the evening of the skipper's anniversary they invited him to a bounteous dinner in the wardroom. The larder had been recently replenished from the captured whalers, and Bulloch, who acted as caterer, superintended the production of a surprisingly fancy birthday dinner, with even a birthday cake. The festivities were unfortunately interrupted by a sudden gale, which brought all hands, including the officers, on deck.

"I knew it!" the cook wailed to the steward, as he looked ruefully at the unfinished dinner on the wardroom table. "I knew we'd have some kind of bad luck. When the cat washed overboard yesterday I told everybody we'd have bad luck. And now, sure enough, here comes this big blow right in the midst of the captain's dinner and ruins everything. Damn that cat!"

Since leaving the Arctic, Captain Waddell had been secretly nursing an audacious idea, a madcap scheme that had entered his mind as at his leisure he reread the captured San Francisco papers. This was before the day of censorship, and the newspapers obligingly printed all the available information on the disposition of the Federal warships—interesting news to a Confederate cruiser's commander.

"Read that over, Mr. Whittle," Waddell said to his chief officer, handing him the paper.

"Very interesting," commented Whittle when he had finished. "It seems there are plenty of enemy warships in the Pacific, but we ought to be able to give them the slip."

"I'm not worrying about them," said the Captain. "But did you notice that there's only one warship, the Saginaw, in San Francisco Bay?"

"What of it? We're not going into San Francisco Bay."

"Why not?" retorted Waddell. "The only protection the city of San Francisco has is that lone cruiser. They're not looking for attack out here."

"But the Saginaw is an ironclad. What chance would a wooden merchantman like the Shenandoah have in a battle with an ironclad warship?"

"That's all right," Waddell replied. "See what the paper says here. The Saginaw is commanded by Charles MacDougal, an old shipmate of mine. I know Mac like a book. He's the finest sort of a fellow personally, but he's mighty fond of his ease. I tell you there's not an officer on this ship as easy-going as MacDougal. I know him."

"Maybe so," agreed Whittle doubtfully, "but his laziness doesn't strengthen our wooden sides. He could sink us like a cracker box."

"He could if we'd let him, but that's not my idea. Here's my plan. Mac is bound to feel a great sense of security, out there far away from the scene of the war. I know he will have grown careless. If we steam into the bay after dark, ram into him at full speed, and throw our full force onto the deck, we'll disarm the watch and get possession of her hatches before they know what's going on. If we act boldly we ought to be able to capture her without the loss of a life. Then the next morning we could train the batteries of the two ships onto the city and have it at our mercy."

"It sounds plausible the way you tell it," Whittle admitted, "but it seems fantastic for us to be planning to capture a big city. It just isn't reasonable."

"Simplest thing in the world. It'll be a good joke on Mac. He'll be surprised to see me on the deck of the Saginaw again. It makes me laugh to think about it."

"It might work out all right," Whittle agreed reluctantly. "Anyhow, we might as well try it."

"The odds are all in our favor," Waddell still insisted. "We'll stop the next ship we see out of San Francisco to learn the latest news there, and if the Saginaw hasn't been reinforced we'll just step in and capture a city."

So they anxiously awaited the sight of an outward bound sail, Waddell and Whittle meanwhile going over their plans for the projected raid and trying to foresee every possible obstacle. At last on August 2 there came from the rigging the old familiar warning of a sail on the horizon. Soon a bark came into clearer sight, and, the wind being light, the cruiser steamed toward her flying the British ensign. As she approached, the bark also showed the British colors. The cruiser stopped her engines, and Bulloch went on board the stranger to verify her nationality and get the latest news from San Francisco.

Within a half hour the small boat returned. As Bulloch came on deck it was obvious from his troubled countenance that he was the bearer of bad news. But, even with the premonitory warnings they had already received, the ship's company were not prepared for the crushing intelligence he brought aboard. The British bark was the Barracouta. She was just thirteen days out of San Francisco, and she had on board newspapers which made it inescapably and undeniably plain that the Southern Confederacy had indeed collapsed. The war had been over since April.

Hardly able to maintain his composure, Captain Waddell sat in his cabin and with troubled face read the accumulation of evil tidings—Lee surrendered, Johnston surrendered, all the armies in the field surrendered, Jefferson Davis in prison in irons. Overwhelming, crushing defeat. There was no getting away from it.

The officers of the Barracouta courteously came on board and expressed their sympathy. But that was all they could do, and having done that, they stood away on their voyage. The Shenandoah was left alone and friendless there in the great Pacific.

Never before in the history of warfare was the commander of a vessel confronted with the problem that now faced Captain Waddell. Not only was he a man without a country; he commanded a ship without a flag.

The possibility of defeat had always lurked in the back of his brain, but he had resolutely refused to entertain the thought of it as a reality. Now, suddenly and unexpectedly, it struck him and he felt strangely unprepared for it. For a long time he sat thinking, his mind in a boiling tumult. Then, rousing himself, he sent for Whittle and, staring vacantly ahead of him, sat waiting.

The news of the Confederacy's collapse had cast a deep and unwonted stillness over the ship's company, and an evil quiet hung over the whole vessel. The click of the door latch sounded strangely loud in the silence of that desolated ship as Lieutenant Whittle came in.

Quickly Whittle looked at the captain appraisingly. Whittle, of all the officers, was closest to Waddell, being his second in command. He knew his commander's weaknesses, but he also knew his strength. He had watched him develop from the irresolution of the early days of the cruise, rising to successive emergencies, and by sheer determination making his first command a successful one. But now his success, by a bit of vagrant and belated bad news, had been transformed into failure. Whittle's ingrained respect for his superior officer was mingled with sympathy for his present plight and apprehension as to how he would react to disaster. Would his resolution be equal to the magnitude of the crisis? Or would the vacillations and uncertainties of the earlier days reappear? The captain gave every outward evidence of serenity.

"A stunning piece of news, Mr. Whittle," he said quietly. "I suppose we won't capture San Francisco after all."

"No sir," the chief officer agreed heavily, hoping his voice would not betray his emotions. "But we'll manage somehow," he finished weakly.

"Mr. Whittle," the Captain went on, "I have a responsibility resting on me now involving not only my own personal honor but the honor of the flag under which we have operated. Our record so far is clean. We must do nothing dishonorable now. But just what course to take I must decide without any precedent. There's nothing in any of the books that covers our predicament."

"I'm confident you will decide only what is right, sir. Whatever course you adopt, I shall support you. You know that."

"The first thing, Mr. Whittle," the Captain said firmly, "beyond any possible question, is to disarm the vessel. We have no right to carry arms now. Will you be good enough to see to that right now? Then I want to talk further with you and the other officers."

Lieutenant Whittle, his own heart heavy, was glad enough to leave the painful atmosphere of the captain's cabin and get to work doing something. Promptly he went about reversing the transformation effected at Madeira nearly a year before. Then it had been the appointed task to convert a merchantman into a cruiser. Now that cruiser must be changed back to a peaceful merchant vessel.

So once more the tackles were got aloft. The guns were dismounted and struck below out of sight. The pistols and rifles and cutlasses were locked away in their chests. The portholes were closed, the smokestack was whitewashed, and in the course of a few days the Shenandoah was a harmless, quiet merchantman, peacefully pursuing her way in all apparent innocence.

CHAPTER EIGHTEEN

THE LAST, LONG,
LONESOME TRIP

L IEUTENANT WHITTLE, the work of disarmament
under way, returned to the captain's cabin,
where the whole complement of commissioned officers
was soon gathered. It was a sober and quiet group
of young men who eyed the sad-faced commander.
Their dream was over. They were no longer hopeful
citizens of a new nation, fighting to establish her
place in the world. Their nation had crumbled from
beneath their feet and left them alone and friendless
in the wide Pacific. What would become of them and
their ship? Which way should they turn? Their bewildered thoughts were brought sharply down to the
immediate problem by the captain's crisp question.

"Well, what shall we do?"

They had been asking themselves that question,
and there had been a variety of answers. Soon there
was a babel of voices in the little cabin as they made
known their views. Some thought they should go
back to England, where they had started from. A
majority, however, felt that the best course would be

to take the ship to Australia and turn her over to the government there, then make their own way back to England as private citizens. Waddell himself was noncommittal while the discussion proceeded, but after the matter had been thoroughly debated he followed the views of the majority and ordered the course changed for Sydney. That seemed the safest and quickest way to end the frustrated cruise. The shadow of the gallows hung over every port of the United States. It was only a question of which neutral haven to seek.

There was not much sleeping on the Shenandoah that night. With the dawning of the new day, there came a deeper realization of the gravity of the situation. They were men without a country. The captain of the Barracouta had told them they were branded as pirates in every port and that the warships of the United States were scouring the seas for the luckless Shenandoah with dire threats as to her fate when she fell into their hands. The poor old "Shenanigan's" luck had run out.

Captain Waddell had stayed awake all night, reflecting on his duty and responsibility in such an emergency. Restlessly he tossed in his bunk as he considered first one phase and then the other. Was he doing right in steaming for Sydney? His judgment told him he should go back to Liverpool. Should he have been swayed by a majority opinion of his officers? And then his stern sense of duty and propriety interjected another question: Was he under an implied obligation of honor to surrender to the United

States? All night he wrestled with these questions, but as the day was breaking he made up his mind. He would go back to Liverpool, surrender to the British authorities, and take the consequences.

Immediately after breakfast the officers were summoned again to his cabin and informed of his change in plans. Those who favored landing in Australia protested against the change. Lee and Bulloch were particularly vehement, but the captain was unmoved by their pleas.

"It would be nonsense," he said, "to take this crew to Australia and set them down there penniless."

Bulloch and Lee were inclined to be insistent, pointing out that a large part of the crew had come from Australia anyway and would be at home when they got there, but would be far from home if taken to Liverpool.

"No!" Waddell finally interrupted them. "There is everything to gain by going to Liverpool, and only imaginary dangers. It will be a long and perhaps a difficult passage. It is 17,000 miles from here to England. The master of the Barracouta tells me that the Yankee warships are warned of our presence and that they are looking everywhere for us. But why can't we avoid observation and escape? We have already traveled more than 40,000 miles without accident. The principal search for us will be made in the Pacific, and so we shall be fairly safe if we can get around the Horn and into the Atlantic. I feel it my duty to surrender the ship and the men to some neutral authority at a point where we shall be accorded the best treatment. I've made up my mind to take this ship to Liverpool, and I'll be damned if I don't take her there."

This seemed positive beyond any possibility of misunderstanding, but before the day was over he called the officers together again for another conference. His mind kept toying with the idea that he was in honor bound to surrender to the United States authorities, and he submitted the suggestion to the officers. Upon arrival at Liverpool, should they surrender to the Yankee consul rather than the British? Or, simpler still, should they steam into New York or some other Yankee port and there surrender and take their medicine?

"My conscience tells me that that is what I should do," he told them, "and I'd do it if I thought you would support me in it." The officers assured him emphatically that they would not support any such suicidal plan, and the meeting adjourned without further discussion.

There was no further discussion in the cabin, but there was plenty of discussion on deck and in the wardroom afterward as the officers got together in little groups to talk about their plight and the captain's indecisive attitude. Bulloch and Lining were standing aft the propeller house thrashing over the matter when the captain came unexpectedly upon them in the midst of their conversation.

"I know what you're talking about!" he said angrily. "You're just a couple of croakers. You think everything I do is wrong. You don't want to go to Liverpool. Well, maybe we won't go to Liverpool.

How would you like to go to New York?" And he walked away.

Bulloch and Lining, alarmed, sought out Whittle and had a long conference with him. Whittle tried to allay their apprehension by telling them that in his opinion they were headed for the Cape of Good Hope, that the captain did not really expect to run the gauntlet of the Atlantic. But Bulloch and Lining were not so easily reassured. They doubted that they were headed for the South African port, but they were not quite sure just where they were going. The captain had first told them Sydney, then had changed to Liverpool, and had suggested New York. The very thought of surrendering to the Yankees chilled their blood. They could detect a strong odor of hemp, and they did not care for it.

Immediately following the encounter with the Barracouta, there was so much excited activity on board, stowing the guns and changing the appearance of the vessel, that the men of the crew had little time to think about their plight. Most of them were mercenaries, British subjects, and the fall of the Southern Confederacy had no emotional or sentimental effect on them. But they did realize that their status was changed with the disappearance of the nation whose flag they flew, and they began to worry about their own safety. After some discussion among themselves they drew up a petition in which they asked the captain to set them down in the nearest British port, although they loyally assured him that, whatever his decision, they would continue to obey his orders. The captain was distraught by the crew's petition, but he realized that the men must be reassured. So the boatswain's whistle shrilled through the ship, the crew was called aft, and when they were gathered there the captain, a little tremor in his voice, spoke to them.

"Men," he said simply, "the war is over. We have been whipped. Our defeat has been crushing and complete. The Southern Confederacy has ceased to exist.

"The first question in your minds, I know, and it's the first question in mine, is about our own personal safety. We have been engaged in a cruise which was projected and prosecuted in good faith. We have struck the commerce of our late enemies blows from which it will not soon recover. That's what we were sent out to do, and we have nothing to be ashamed of. But that's all behind us now. We've got to look to the future.

"One thing is certain. As a cruiser we no longer have any right to sail the seas. In such a character we would be liable to capture by the ship of any civilized nation, for we no longer have a flag to give legality to any warlike activities. I have therefore had the vessel disarmed, and will proceed with plans to set you ashore at some safe and convenient place on British soil. Don't worry. I'll get you safely home somehow. You stick to me and I'll stand by you."

This somewhat equivocal utterance was construed by some of the men as meaning that they would make for Australia, but their minds were disabused of this fancy as they continued on their way and the sun still rose over the port rail. But the men shrugged their shoulders and went about their tasks with no more petitions, and no more grumbling than they ordinarily did among themselves. And there was no more disaffection among them, at any rate, than there was among the officers.

Most of the officers, to be sure, did not permit their worries to affect their work. Dr. McNulty, however, began more and more to seek consolation in the bottle. At length one day—the day they crossed the Equator for the third time—he appeared on deck rip-staving drunk and totally unfit for duty.

"Perhaps I'll have to disrate him," Waddell said to Lining. "Apparently he can't stay sober. Can you get along without him?"

"I certainly can," responded Lining, who was weary of his bibulous assistant. But the captain's resolution was insufficient, and the assistant surgeon's public drunkenness continued unpunished.

"The captain's getting more wishy-washy than ever," said one of the officers one night as they sat about the table in the wardroom drinking a final night-cap.

"Not only that, but he's a sorry sailor," said another. "Take a look at the merchantmen we pass. They all carry more sail than we do."

"The skipper says he's afraid to crowd on more sail. Says when night comes on he keeps thinking of the danger of squalls coming up and he just has to take in sail."

"That's a fine kind of a captain that's afraid to

put on sail," commented Scales. "Let me get in two or three drinks and I'll carry sail till everything is blue," and he downed another glass.

Perhaps the officers sat too long about the table that night. At any rate, Scales overslept the next morning and did not come to quarters, thus precipitating another crisis which quickly threatened to disrupt the whole personnel. Waddell, in dealing with Scales, admitted the changed relationship since receiving the news of the end of the war.

"I am now only the master of the ship," he said, "and no longer the commander of a man-of-war. I have no right to punish you, but I am forced to relieve you of all duty. You are now no longer an officer on this ship, but you may consider yourself a passenger at large until we get into port."

To make a bad matter worse, Waddell assigned Blacker, the clerk, to keep Scales's watch. Thereupon Hunt refused to serve under Blacker, with whom he had a private feud, and Hunt was ordered also to consider himself a passenger and no longer an officer. Blacker, unwilling to be a bone of contention, refused to serve on the watch, whereupon Waddell, with an air of injured dignity, announced that he would take Scales's place on deck. This was too much for Bulloch's sense of propriety, and he went to Waddell and volunteered to stand the watch himself.

"It doesn't look well for the captain of a ship to be keeping watch when there are so many officers aboard," he said.

The next morning Scales, after spending the night considering the matter, arrived at the conclusion that he had been mistreated and took himself to the captain's cabin to unbosom himself.

"You have been looking for a long while for an excuse to put me off the deck," he told him bitterly, "and you jumped at yesterday's opportunity to do so. You simply wanted to humiliate me. It is utterly ridiculous to attach so much importance to so small an offense—to break an officer for oversleeping. And another thing. I don't want you to think that I'm under any obligation to you for passage home. If you consider it an obligation, I'll go forward, peel off my coat, and work with the men for my passage. I want no favors from you, sir."

Having delivered himself of this tirade, Scales stalked out of the cabin without waiting for a reply, but the next day he was restored to duty. Hunt meanwhile had attempted to ignore his disrating and reported for duty, but was told sharply that his services could be dispensed with. Hunt, who had a surly streak, had his revenge by spreading a report among the men that when the voyage was over they would be paid only a shilling on the pound, a canard which had the desired effect of producing great discontent and hard talking among the crew.

An evil genius seemed to haunt the ship at this time. Even the reliable Smith Lee was on the carpet —the first time he had ever been in trouble since he had been in the Navy. His offense was smoking on duty while standing the morning watch. Whittle caught him redhanded and reprimanded him harshly. This aroused Lee's ire, and he defiantly proclaimed, "All hell can't make me leave off my pipe." Haled before the captain, he continued his defiant attitude and absolutely refused to comply with Waddell's request for a promise not to smoke on duty in the future.

"Without such a promise I shall have to relieve you from duty," the captain threatened.

"That's all right with me," Lee retorted, and Bulloch was forthwith assigned to his watch.

Next day the captain sent for all the watch officers and explained the state of affairs to them. To keep Bulloch in Lee's place, he pointed out, would punish Bulloch rather than Lee, so he had decided to put them into three watches of longer hours each. Grimball thereupon volunteered the opinion that Lee was right in refusing to have a promise extorted from him under threat of punishment. He added that he himself smoked on watch and if he was caught at it expected merely to be punished for it and returned to duty. Scales likewise confessed that he smoked at pleasure during the long night watches, and intended to continue doing so. The captain was thunderstruck by these developments and, saying nothing more, dismissed the officers. The ultimate outcome was that Lee was restored to duty, and the captain attempted to save his face by issuing a written order that officers must not smoke on duty.

There were now only anxious and troubled faces in wardroom and forecastle. The lookouts still mounted aloft, but it was not to scan the horizon hopefully for enemy ships that might be captured. The principal object in view now was carefully to avoid all other vessels. Off the coast of South America, several American merchantmen were sighted on westerly courses, but they were given a wide berth. The only vessel encountered which was standing to the east, as was the Shenandoah, was a British ship, and the Britisher, to the immense chagrin of the Shenandoah's men, showed them a clean pair of heels and soon passed out of sight, although the cruiser had crowded on all sail and was making twelve or thirteen knots.

Waddell was troubled by this episode. It was the first time any vessel had demonstrated an ability to outrun his ship, a matter of pride to any skipper, but there was more than mere pride involved now, when they might be forced to match speed with a pursuer at any minute.

"I suppose it's the condition of the copper on our bottom," he said to Whittle. "She's probably covered with barnacles a foot thick. And that's bad. We'll need all her fleetness if we have to run before a Yankee cruiser."

The captain having brought up the subject, Whittle was emboldened to raise the question which had been so thoroughly debated in the wardroom: Why didn't he put on more sail? At length the captain was persuaded to put the mainsail on her, and when the reel was held she was found to be making sixteen knots. Waddell was amazed at her speed.

"Why, that's faster than I ever saw the ship go before," he exclaimed with a note of pride in his voice. Then at once the conservative side of his nature asserted itself, and he began to worry about whether to leave the extra canvas on her at night.

"Do you think you can sleep with the topgallant sails and mainsail on her?" he asked.

"Yes," said Whittle, who was growing impatient at the captain's timidity, "even if you put the spanker on her." Waddell was by no means reassured, but Dr. Lining, who was treating the captain for a crick in his neck, prescribed a hot toddy for him and put him to bed and to sleep.

With full sail left on all night and next day, the cruiser made her best day's run, 260 miles, and the captain began to feel a little more cheerful. But everybody's nerves were raveling out now. Scales, seeking a more comfortable mode of sleeping, had a hammock made and got the permission of the officers to swing it in the wardroom. As soon as Waddell saw it, he made Scales take it down.

"It will interfere with my passing through," he said imperiously. The officers were unanimous in resenting this invasion of their demesne by the commander.

"He has no right to give such an order," Scales complained hotly. "If the Navy still existed I'd be justified in filing a formal protest with Secretary Mallory."

But the chorus of agreement was silenced when the saturnine Dr. Lining reminded them, "But the Navy has all busted up. There's not any more Navy except the poor old 'Shenanigan,' and she's running for her life."

The hammock incident intensified Scales's sulky disdain for the captain, but there were no more untoward incidents in the run from the Line to the Cape. Once fairly started around the Horn, however, on September 16 they got a full dose of that furious weather which long ago led the sailors to call it "Old Cape Misery." The officers and men were just congratulating themselves on their safe passage around this always treacherous point when almost without warning they ran into a gale which for a few hours was phenomenally terrific. Although the ship lay to under close-reefed main-topsail and fore-stay-sail with a tarpaulin in the rigging to ride it out, her speed could not be held under five knots.

Captain Waddell deemed it more prudent to go ahead than to heave to, even under the adverse conditions, for he was in a strong easterly current and none too certain of his whereabouts, as he had been without observations for several days. So the ship plunged ahead, more or less blindly, fighting mountainous seas day and night which dashed their icy spray far into the rigging and time and again tumbled such enormous quantities of water on the deck as to make her reel and shudder under the shock. The nights brought a Stygian blackness, not a mere absence of light, but a seemingly palpable darkness which closed down on the ship with the pressure of a deadening weight. The lanterns flickered uncertainly, as though struggling to penetrate the surrounding gloom; and the steersman at the wheel stared fearfully ahead as they rushed along the dark and unfamiliar way.

As the ship skirted the antarctic waters, she was

247

again subjected to the threat of giant icebergs, the Captain having chosen a course much farther to the south than is ordinarily taken by vessels rounding the Cape to avoid falling in with any inquisitive vessels. Even with all their experience in the Arctic Ocean, these southern icebergs sometimes terrified the men as they loomed out of the night in all their castellated majesty, rearing their spiked heads hundreds of feet in the air and, by their towering altitude, giving evidence of the menace of their great bulk under water. The men on deck spent their time speculating on the probable height of the islands of ice as they sailed silently by, until the industrious and inquisitive Hunt got out a sextant and by computation announced that the one he measured was 320 feet from the water to its pinnacle.

But at last that dangerous passage was completed. Out again in the open Atlantic, the steamer's course was northward with a good southeast trade wind. She crossed her outward track on September 25 in 30° south latitude, thus completing her circumnavigation of the globe, then straightened out for the dash to Liverpool.

The worst of the return trip seemed to be over, but there were still six thousand miles to be traversed before Liverpool was reached, and the terrifying swing around Cape Horn had further upset the composure of some of the officers. The strain of failure, defeat, and blind flight from an unseen but constantly threatening foe was beginning to undermine their equanimity. Men in knots of twos and threes might be seen with their heads together on deck or in the wardroom, with worried looks on their faces which gave foreboding of the panicky apprehension which was beginning to brew in some minds.

Was the captain right in stubbornly persisting in his determination to proceed to Liverpool? Who knew what dangers might lie ahead? The Atlantic was probably swarming with Yankee cruisers. How would it fare with them if they were captured and thrown into Northern prisons to be tried for piracy in the military courts of a victorious enemy? It takes a brave man not to flinch at the prospect of a rope around his neck. And even if they escaped capture, was the Shenandoah after all her buffeting in condition to brave the storms which customarily raged in the North Atlantic during the months just ahead? Did she have enough coal if it should become necessary to make steam?

"Who was it that said we were going to Cape Town?" asked Bulloch. "It ought to be plain to anybody now that we're not going there. I believe the captain's determined to keep on sailing until we get captured—or shipwrecked."

"As far as I'm concerned," retorted Grimball, "I'd rather be captured and in prison twenty years than to be set down to rot in Cape Town. I want to get closer to home than that."

"You'll probably be captured all right if we keep on for Liverpool," the gloomy O'Brien shot back at him. "That is, if you don't go to the bottom in a gale. As for me, I hope we may be captured if that hard-headed fool persists in taking us into those North Atlantic storms. It would serve him right.

Anyhow, I'd rather be captured than drowned."

Scales, surprisingly enough, supported Waddell's course. "The captain has made a lot of mistakes," he said, "but he's right about this. I wouldn't want to go sneaking into Cape Town."

"Sneaking into Cape Town!" Bulloch repeated hotly. "What's the difference between sneaking into Cape Town and sneaking into Liverpool? If we're not going back to some place like Charleston or Wilmington, why don't we go to the nearest English port like we were promised? I think it's foolish to take the risk of the long trip to Liverpool, and I think we ought to let the captain know how we feel about it."

"Why don't you draw up a letter or a petition, then?" Chew asked him. "I'll sign it with you, and a lot of the others will, too, I know."

"I don't mind writing it if there's enough of you willing to sign it," Bulloch assented. Accordingly he withdrew to his cabin and spent a laborious evening in composition, and on the morning of September 28 summoned the dissenters. Aside from Bulloch, there were two other survivors of the Alabama, Paymaster Smith and Engineer O'Brien. Also there were Chew and Lining and Midshipman Browne. They were very much in earnest as they gathered around the table where Bulloch was seated.

"We've got ourselves to look out for, men," he told them earnestly. "We don't want to be hanged, and we don't want to be shipwrecked either, and Captain Waddell ought to be told how we feel about it. Now here's the letter I've written to him—putting down in writing the things we've been saying to one another.

If we all sign it, it may make him change his mind. Liverpool's all right, and I wish I was there right now, but Cape Town's not far away and I'd rather take my chances there instead of trying to get back to England. Listen to what I've written.

"Sir: In consideration of the unparalleled state of affairs, we have taken the liberty of respectfully laying this communication before you, to convey to you the anxiety and regret with which we regard the prospect of a passage in this ship, under the altered circumstances in which she is placed, to a country so distant as England. So long as we had a country and a government to support and sustain us, it was done cheerfully and with alacrity; so long as there was an object to be gained, that object was sought for by none more eagerly than ourselves; so long even as this ship herself was engaged in cruising, none co-operated with her more zealously than ourselves. Now, we respectfully submit, all these motives for exertion are gone. Our country and government have by the sad fortunes of war ceased to exist . . ."

And so on, in sounding phrases, Bulloch recounted the plight of the vessel in which they found themselves. "Being parties interested to the last degree in this question, we have deemed it a duty to ourselves to lay before you, not for your guidance, but for your impartial consideration, the reasons which have appeared to us so cogent." Here Bulloch's letter insisted that they be landed at the nearest and most convenient port. They suggested Cape Town, only two thousand miles away.

"We regard with proper horror," went on Bulloch's epistle, "any prospect of capture or imprisonment at this late day." And then there was a suggestion of the danger of shipwreck, and another pointed reference to the right of every man to make his own decision as to what was best for his own personal welfare, closing with the milder statement, "We feel sure that you will do us the justice to attribute this letter to its proper motive, viz., a sense of duty, and not an intention of casting any disrespect upon yourself. We distinctly disclaim any intention or desire to trammel your judgment or interfere with your functions."

"That hits the spot," agreed the fiery Dr. Lining. "You've expressed my sentiments exactly."

But at the last moment a persisting spark of loyalty flared up in the youthful Browne's heart.

"Is it right," he asked timorously, "for a subordinate officer to address a letter like that to his captain? Saying we are not trying to interfere with his functions doesn't change the fact that we are doing that very thing. We're objecting to what he's doing. Isn't that sort of like mutiny?"

"It might be, under normal conditions," the plausible Bulloch agreed. "But these are not normal conditions. There can't be any mutiny unless there's some authority to mutiny against. And, as for the captain, answer me this: What's he captain of? His commission was issued by the Confederate States, and now there's not any Confederate States. He's got no real authority over anybody any longer."

"Don't say that too loud," urged O'Brien. "I wouldn't like for the men of the crew to get it in their heads that the officers have no authority. They could cause us trouble if they chose to get ugly."

Bulloch vigorously advocated the signing and dispatch of the protest and, the misgivings of the others allayed, the six of them at length signed the extraordinary letter, with Chew's name heading the list. Along with it went to the captain a similar letter from a group of the steerage and forward officers, probably inspired by one of Bulloch's group.

"The ship," this letter began, "has now arrived at a position where we feel the urgent necessity of impressing you with our feelings as to the destination," and forthwith they expressed their view that Cape Town should be that destination instead of Liverpool. Cape Town was now so near that the passage there would occupy only ten or fourteen days, whereas to go on to England would take forty days at the least. In Cape Town, they felt sure, they would be greeted with sympathy and afforded a means of making their way home on some of the mail boats or Calcutta steamers. On the other hand, they said, proceeding through the North Atlantic would expose them to two grave risks, capture and shipwreck.

"As this ship has gained for herself great notoriety," they pointed out, "we may very readily conclude that ships are already on the lookout for us on the usual route, and no other one can we adopt on account of the scarcity of our fuel. We can not reasonably expect any good treatment if we fall into the hands of the United States government. Their treatment of prisoners has already shown sufficiently how we may be dealt with." As to the ship itself, they

advanced the opinion that having used up most of
her coal she was already so light as to be almost un-
seaworthy, and they expressed grave fears that the
vessel would be unfit and unable to contend with
"the furious weather that constantly prevails on the
British coasts from November to April. Here the
lives of all on board will be placed in more jeopardy
than their liberties, and we entreat you to seriously
weigh over these considerations." They concluded by
requesting, even if the captain decided not to put in
at Cape Town, that he give them an opportunity of
landing at some of the bays along the coast of Africa
"which we would infinitely prefer to the chances of
capture or shipwreck."

This remarkable communication was signed by
William H. Codd, John Hutchinson, and Ernest
Maguffeney, assistant engineers; J. F. Minor, Lodge
Colton, and Thomas S. Manning, acting master's
mates; Henry Alcott, the sailmaker; J. C. Lynch, as-
sistant carpenter; J. C. Blacker, and G. P. Canning.

Captain Waddell was not entirely unaware of the
disaffection among the men on board. In his cabin he
could not avoid being an involuntary eavesdropper as
the arguments in the wardroom raged. But he was
surprised and incensed by the receipt of these communications from members of his official staff. Furthermore, misled by the fact that Chew's name
headed the list of signatures, he leaped to the conclusion that the hapless Chew had inspired and
authored the letter, and it added to his indignation to
think that the leader in the insubordination should

be the officer he considered the least competent. He
fumed as he read the letter over and over.

Such a communication from his officers, of course,
could not be ignored, but at the same time he was determined not to be influenced by their wishes. Pre-
sumably those who did not sign the petition were in
agreement with his views, but he could not be positive about that. Whittle, for instance, had shown
that he was none too enthusiastic about going to
Liverpool. If he called a conference of all his officers
to advise him, the dissenters would probably outvote
his supporters, and he did not propose to take any
such chance as that. He was going to Liverpool, officers or no officers, but he would like to have it ap-
pear that a majority of them agreed with him in that
course. In his perplexity and desperation he resorted
to the dubious device of calling a sort of rump council
of the officers consisting of a group carefully selected
to give his supporters a safe majority. Whittle was
included; despite his doubts as to Whittle, he could
not omit his first officer from any such advisory
council. Chew was called, to give color of representa-
tion to the Cape Town faction. But, to be entirely
on the safe side, the only others invited to the meeting
were Grimball, Lee, and Scales, all of whom, from
the overheard conversations, he knew to be favorable
to the Liverpool course.

With his handpicked jury assembled in his cabin,
the captain submitted his case.

"Frankly," he told them, "I originally intended to
go to Cape Town, as I told you, Mr. Whittle. After

rounding Cape Horn, however, I changed my mind
and decided that it was advisable to go to Liverpool
instead. It is my judgment that such is our safest
course. But, in view of the extraordinary letter I
have received today from a few malcontents" (with a
glare at Chew) "I have decided to seek your advice
and be guided by your decision. It will please me if
you will express your views and I assure you that I
will be governed by the majority vote."

So, solemnly, they cast their ballots. Grimball,
Lee and Scales, as expected, voted in favor of Liverpool. Chew stuck out for Cape Town, and Whittle,
not entirely to Waddell's surprise, supported Chew.

"Well, gentlemen," the captain declared unctu-
ously, "you have decided. Liverpool it is. You may go
now—all but you, Mr. Whittle. I wish to see you, Mr.
Whittle."

The others gone, Waddell turned angrily to his
chief officer.

"I'm surprised to find you supporting such a
mutinous movement, Mr. Whittle," he said with a
great display of heat. "It's mutiny! That's what it is,
mutiny. I ought to string every one of them to a
yardarm, and if I had a government back of me I'd
do it. Who ever heard of such effrontery—telling
their captain what he ought to do! They know I'm
in a unique position, and they're trying to take advantage of it. But it's mutiny, just the same."

"It's unusual, to be sure," Whittle agreed im-
perturbably, "but I believe 'mutiny' is too strong a
word, if you please. I didn't consider it proper for me,
the first officer, to sign the letter of protest, but I

agree with those who did sign it. I don't think we should risk the hazardous passage to Liverpool, and I don't blame those who feel the same way and have had the courage to speak out and assert themselves."

"Well, I don't care how they feel," exclaimed Waddell. "I'm still captain of this ship. The ship and everybody on her were placed under my authority when we started out and they'll stay under my authority until we get back to port—a port of my choosing. I'm still captain, and I'm not afraid of Yankee cruisers or storms. What's more, my judgment has been supported by a majority vote of the council, and I'm going ahead."

Waddell paused for a moment.

"You've got the arms under lock and key?"

Whittle nodded silently.

"And you might be inquiring about cautiously to see which of the men are still loyal. I hope it doesn't come to an open outbreak or to bloodshed, but I'm going to Liverpool, Mr. Whittle."

"I don't think there's any danger from the crew," Whittle assured him. "But I'll be on the lookout for any sign of trouble. As long as I'm on board, I know my duty is to my ship and to my captain. Regardless of my own views, I'll carry out your orders and support your judgment as captain. It's only fair to say, however, that I attach no importance at all to the verdict of a packed jury." And the captain said nothing as his first lieutenant left the cabin.

That was a wretched night for Captain Waddell. Bitter thoughts crowded his mind. After a lifetime spent on the seas, his first command was ending in defeat and mutinous mutterings. He read the letters over and over. He scanned the names attached to them. And Whittle, too! He knew Whittle's loyalty could be depended on, but he was regretful to find their views at variance. And he resented that taunting reference to a packed jury—resented it but could not deny it. Perhaps it had been a mistake not to include all the officers, as usual, in the council, Bulloch and Lining and all of them. Perhaps they would have outvoted him—but maybe, after all, he ought to go to Cape Town. Perhaps—he dozed off into a troubled sleep.

The next morning his composure was to some extent restored when Grimball walked into the Captain's cabin and deferentially handed him a formal letter.

"Sir: It was not our original intention to address you on the subject of the future destination of the Shenandoah, but since you have received two communications, signed by most of the officers of the ship, expressing views and opinions in direct opposition to those entertained by yourself, viz., your intention to take the ship to some port in England or France, it will be a source of gratification for us to know that in connection with those documents you have also this one, which expresses our unqualified approbation of the course you have determined upon. Be the fortunes of war and shipwreck in our passage (which appears to excite so much uneasiness in some) what they may, we consider either England or France the only proper destination for the Shenandoah."

This brief but comforting note was signed by Grimball, Lee, Scales, Surgeon McNulty, and Midshipman Mason. Along with it there was delivered to the captain's cabin an even more pleasing and heartening communication signed by 71 of the 110 members of the crew:

"Sir, We, the undersigned petty officers and men of the C. S. S. Shenandoah, take the liberty of writing this petition in consequence of a certain paper, purporting to be the petition of the crew, having been formerly laid before you. Sir, in complete denial of this paper and its object, and of petitioning you on such a subject whatsoever, and to show our complete reliance and trust in whatever it should please you to do under any circumstances is the earnest and sincere feeling which has caused us to lay this before you.

"Trusting our intention will be our excuse, we remain, sir, your most humble servants—" and then followed the names of the loyal members of the crew, scrawled in varying degrees of legibility at the foot of the paper.

The receipt of these expressions of loyalty was a tonic to the troubled spirit of the distraught commander. His confidence restored, he determined to rebuke the dissenters by reprimanding their supposed leader. So, summoning Lieutenant Chew to his cabin, he bade him be seated.

"Mr. Chew," he said, "you have been guilty of the gravest breach of discipline and decorum. You can not plead ignorance. You have attended the Academy, where respect for your superiors is the first lesson. Under anything like ordinary conditions you should be put under arrest, you and those who joined you in signing this disgraceful letter!" And he emphasized his indignation by slapping the offending letter with the palm of his hand.

"But," he continued, "I am making allowances for our unusual position. I want to be fair. I realize that you have weakly permitted your fears to upset your judgment. But I want you to know that not all the men on this ship share your fears. I have been favored with two other letters. Let me read them to you, Mr. Chew."

Then, when he had finished reading them, he exclaimed:

"Mull that over, Mr. Chew! You see I still have some loyal officers and men left, brave men not afraid of capture or disaster. Now go back and give your fellow mutineers this message: I am still the captain of this ship, and I will take her to Liverpool or die on her deck. That's all, Mr. Chew."

The bewildered Chew withdrew, all unaware of the reason for his being singled out for rebuke, but he duly reported to Bulloch and the others that their letters had had no effect.

The drafting of the various communications to the captain had developed a sharp cleavage of the officers into two distinct cliques, and as they sat glumly around the supper table in the wardroom that night there was little badinage or crossfire of conversation. Waddell, having asserted his authority and justified his course, had his good nature restored, and he bethought himself to assuage the ruffled feelings of his officers by the proffer of an olive branch in bottled form. So as they sat there in constrained silence, they were surprised to receive from the commander a bottle of champagne, with the suggestion that, as the ship had now been around the world, they should drink to that event.

"Well, I'll not drink any of his champagne," blurted out Bulloch, "and especially not in honor of his circumnavigating the globe. That's the only reason why we're not safely in Sydney right now—the captain is so vain he wanted to be able to say he commanded the only Confederate warship that went all around the world. Just to feed his vanity he risks our lives and defies the judgment of his officers. To hell with his champagne!" And he left the wardroom angrily, slamming the door behind him.

Dr. Lining, surprisingly, sought to pour oil on the water.

"Mr. Bulloch is too hasty," he said gently. "I think the captain's course is wrong, but his sending us the champagne is kindly and politely meant. Let us all join in the toast." So they rose and drank (some of them rather dourly) "To the Shenandoah— she has carried the Confederate flag around the world." But, though they drank the toast together, they finished their meal in sullen silence, the invisible wall of dissension effectively dividing the two factions.

On October 11 the Shenandoah crossed the Line, and those who had been aboard on the outward trip could not avoid reflecting on the contrast of this crossing with that jollification when King Neptune had come aboard nearly a year before in search of his unchristened subjects. Gone now was the ebullience and the hopeful anticipation which had pervaded the vessel at that time. Not only were they bearing the heavy weight of failure and defeat, but they were enervated now by privation and sickness.

Not only was there the increasing possibility of a food shortage, but worse, the carefully guarded supply of fresh water was running low, and the Captain had found it necessary to put the whole personnel on short water rations in order to make it last until the vessel could get back to Liverpool. A half pint of water a day is not much, especially under the burning sun of the tropics, and there was real suffering and distress as the ship made its way through the sun-burnished equatorial seas. To add to their load of physical woes, there was an outbreak of scurvy on board, and a sick bay was improvised in the forecastle for the care of the sallow, emaciated men who found it impossible to stay on their feet.

"I feared as much," Dr. Lining said sadly, in reporting the bad news to the Captain. "We have gone for months, you know, without fresh vegetables of any kind. The human constitution can stand just so much of this limited diet and no more. I'm doing the best I can, sir, but the men are in bad shape. And my medicines won't do them much good—what they need is onions and lemons and cabbages."

In latitude 10° north the Shenandoah took the northeast trade wind. Although the lookouts sighted a number of distant sails from time to time, she kept at a respectful distance from them and continued slowly working her way along through the doldrums under sail. On the afternoon of October 25, about 400 miles southeast of the Azores, when she·had crossed the trade belt and was running out of the northern edge of it in light air, the masthead lookout cried out, "Sail ho!"

The cry, once so welcome on board the raiding cruiser, brought only apprehension now. Every sail sighted might be one of the dreaded Federal warships. Glasses now swept the northern horizon in anxious search of the stranger, but she was still so far away as to be visible only from aloft. Captain Waddell, thoroughly alive to the danger, sent a quartermaster above with instructions to communicate to him whatever he could ascertain from the appearance of the sail.

"She's under short sail," he reported, "with her mainsail up or furled. From the spread of her masts she appears to be a steamer, though she's still too far away to tell for certain. She's standing a little more to the east of north than we're heading."

The report sounded ominous. A steamer in those waters was more than likely a cruiser, and a cruiser in that locality would have but one probable objective, to waylay the Shenandoah.

"We've got to be careful what we do here, Mr. Whittle," Captain Waddell remarked anxiously. "The sun is still thirty minutes high. She's doubtless watching us, as we are watching her, and we must be sure not to excite suspicion while we are still visible."

"Yes, sir," replied Whittle. "It would be fatal to change our course or to crowd on more sail while we're under observation. They'd be right on top of us if we tried to get away, wanting to investigate us."

"And that's the last thing we want," interrupted the captain. "We'll continue to breeze along, just as we are, until nightfall. Then we'll see what can be done about it. Maybe we can make the darkness our ally here. It's our only chance of concealment."

After the sun had gone down, but while there was still plenty of light, the quartermaster was sent aloft again to observe the stranger, and this time his report was even more alarming.

"She's a cruiser all right, sir. She seems to be waiting in order to speak to us."

The Federal warship was now fairly visible from the deck, and every officer and man not otherwise employed crowded the rail and watched her with fearful fascination. After nearly fifty thousand miles of safe cruising, it would be heartbreaking to be captured here on the last lap of the voyage.

Captain Waddell paced the deck in a fever of suspense.

"Did you ever see the darkness come so slowly?" he asked impatiently of Lieutenant Grimball, who stood at his side. "And darkness is our only hope. Our security, if any remains at all, depends on maintaining an appearance of innocence, strictly adhering to our present course as long as we can be seen. Any deviation would instantly arouse suspicion. On the other hand, we are lost if we get up within speaking distance of her while it's still light. Only the night can save us now."

As though fearing no danger, the Shenandoah

swept forward steadily toward the Federal cruiser patiently and confidently waiting there for her prey. Every minute the distance between them was lessened. Every minute the danger increased.

"She's only four miles away now, sir," announced the quartermaster, and the captain's features tightened as he waited silently at the rail. But hardly had the ominous report been made than the brief tropical twilight came to its sudden close, and the friendly darkness raised its barrier of safety between the two vessels.

Once in the sheltering obscurity of the night, all was action on the Shenandoah. Swiftly her head was turned sharply eastward, and steam was ordered up. It was the first time she had been under steam since leaving the equator in the Pacific, and it took two hours to get the engines going, but by nine o'clock, when the moon rose, her sails had been furled, decreasing her visibility, and she was steaming at full speed away from the lurking enemy. Fortunately she was burning Cardiff coal, which gave off only a light smoke invisible beyond two hundred yards, and now that the engines were working and the steamer was headed to the east, a feeling of security returned.

Throughout all that night she steamed eastward and then, the danger apparently averted, she resumed her course to Liverpool while the men, the tension relieved, laughed at the mystification they must have caused the Yankee warship when they slipped around her in the night. With the return of daylight she was put under sail, but the next night she was steaming again, and thus zigzagged her way

in the direction of her haven, using the friendly night
to elude chance watchers of the daylight hours.

The Shenandoah had been at sea for more than a
year without the loss of a man from any cause. But
now, as they drew near to the end of their long
voyage, death came among them for the first time.
There were two sick men on board, Sergeant Canning
and "William Bill," one of the Kanakas. Although
they hung on tenaciously, it was obvious that both
were near the end. McLaren, the master-at-arms,
said with a callous jest that the death angel was just
hovering above the rigging until he could carry off
two at once.

"Old Square Foot don't like to make two trips
where one will serve. He'll pick 'em both up some
day soon." But McLaren was wrong. Old Square
Foot had to make two trips after all. William Bill,
wasted with disease, went first, and the ship had its
first burial at sea. There was not much ceremony
about it. Captain Waddell read the burial service
from the prayer book, and the body of the friendless
South Sea Islander was dropped from the poop deck
into the waters of the Atlantic.

Poor George Canning shuddered as he witnessed
the solemn scene. For two weeks he had been unable to
leave his bed, slowly wasting away. A week before,
his bunk had been brought on deck so he could get
more fresh air, and there he was ensconced under the
boat, protected from the sun and rain and spray by a
tarpaulin.

"I may not last out the voyage," he had said when

he joined the crew at Melbourne—a gloomy but well-founded foreboding. Throughout the whole cruise he had suffered with that bullet hole through his lungs, a wound which defied Dr. Lining's best efforts to heal. Then, in his weakened condition, he had been among the first to fall a victim to scurvy. He was patiently tended during his last days by Edward Weeks, an old Negro who had formed a strong attachment for Mister George, but his condition had not been considered immediately precarious until the very night of his death. Then, after lying silent for an hour or more, he reached out suddenly and took the faithful old Negro's hand.

"Good-bye, Weeks," he said feebly. "I'm going. Take care of yourself, old fellow." And he was dead.

That night Canning's emaciated body was stitched in his canvas hammock, to the foot of which two thirty-two pound cannonballs were sewed. The next morning there wailed through the ship the shrill sound of the boatswain's pipe with its eerie summons of "all hands on deck to bury the dead."

The whole ship's company slowly assembled on deck with shuffling feet and serious faces. The body lay on a smooth plank, one end on the taffrail and the other supported by two sober-faced sailors. All heads were uncovered as Dr. McNulty, prayer book in hand, read the solemn burial service of the Roman Catholic Church of which he and Canning were fellow-members. As the surgeon spoke the words, "We therefore commit his body to the deep, looking for the general resurrection in the last day, when the earth and sea shall give up their dead," the inner end of the plank was tilted upward. All that was mortal of poor Canning plunged into the water with a pitiful little splash, amid a silence unbroken except by a sob from the heartbroken Weeks and the requiem of the wind whistling through the rigging.

It might have been more fitting if Canning's burial service had been read by Dr. Lining instead of McNulty. The death of the poor, suffering man probably meant more to Lining than it did to any man on board, with the possible exception of the dusky Weeks. It was not that the surgeon was particularly fond of Canning personally. In fact, he was inclined to be critical of Canning's taciturnity and irritability. But personalities did not enter into it. It was purely a matter of professional pride.

"What a pity!" he said to Grimball as he gazed sadly over the rail. "God knows I did my best to keep him alive. It was my ambition to complete the cruise without losing a single man from sickness, and I almost made it. It was bad enough for that Kanaka to die, but I wouldn't have counted that. But Canning. Too bad the poor chap wasn't a man of stronger physique."

But this was to be not the worst of Dr. Lining's worries during those last few weeks of the voyage. And, as was not unusual, the trouble started with his undependable assistant, Dr. McNulty. The prologue to the drama had a familiar setting—McNulty got drunk and had a row with Blacker. The brawl might have had no serious consequences, but Mc-

Nulty went a step too far and deliberately and grossly insulted his brother-Irishman—called him, in fact, "a bloody English-Irish Orangeman." Ordinarily a man of peace, Blacker could not swallow this. No deadlier insult could be offered an Irishman, the offending epithets involving religion, politics, and a deadly internecine feud. Blacker rushed to Whittle to report the matter.

"I don't like to be a tale-bearer," he apologized, "but there's a limit to what a man can stand."

Whittle thereupon sought out McNulty and ordered him to go to his cabin to sober up and to stay there until he was given permission to come out. McNulty was in such an obstinate state that he refused to go. When Whittle advanced on him he unexpectedly whipped a pistol out of his pocket and flourished it uncertainly and cried dramatically, "Stand back, sir! Don't come a step closer."

Whittle, however, not intimidated by this show of resistance, speedily disarmed the inebriated surgeon and had him sent below.

The next day, when McNulty had sobered up, and Waddell had him on the deck, he amazed everybody by denying that he had been drunk or that he had threatened the first officer. He had drawn the pistol from his pocket, he said, to show it to Whittle and ask his opinion as to its quality. Elaborating his defense, he volunteered the statement that the reason he quarreled with Blacker in the first place was that Blacker had abused the captain in his presence and he would not tolerate it.

"I could not stand there and endure his black-guarding you, sir," he told Waddell, with a quaver in his voice.

The captain, however, was not taken in by this transparent appeal to his vanity, and McNulty's story was discredited by all the witnesses. Whittle was particularly emphatic in his indignation at McNulty's mendacity and flat-footedly accused him of lying.

"Well, sir," returned McNulty, with the elaborate gravity of postintoxication, "when we get on shore there is a way of settling all these things."

"Very well," Whittle readily assented, "I am willing, at any time and place."

"Do you waive all rank?"

"Yes, and I will give you any satisfaction." McNulty walked off.

"Do you suppose that drunken fool really means to challenge me?" Whittle asked Lining, who had been a witness to the interview.

"Oh, no. That's the last of it, you may be sure. McNulty hasn't spunk enough to fight a duel. He was just trying to talk big."

Next morning, however, as Whittle was sitting in his cabin, Smith Lee walked in with unaccustomed gravity and formally presented him with a note from McNulty demanding a retraction "or the satisfaction one gentleman might expect from another." Whittle was taken aback by this, and sent Scales to ask Lining to come to his cabin.

"I have nothing to withdraw," Whittle told the doctor. "McNulty told a lie. I said he did, and I couldn't possibly say he didn't. If he insists on fighting, I'll accommodate him. I believe it is customary for each principal in such an affair to have a 'friend' or second. Will you serve me in that capacity?"

Lining gladly accepted, and advised Whittle to write Lee, who was serving as McNulty's friend, that the ship was not the proper place to settle such things, but that he would be glad to give McNulty full satisfaction when they got ashore. Whittle pointed out, however, that Lee had told him that McNulty insisted that the matter must be settled then and there, without delay.

"Well," Scales reminded him, "you promised to give him satisfaction 'any time or place' and you can't avoid doing it now, even on the ship, if McNulty demands it. I know the code, and that's according to the code."

"Very well," Whittle agreed impatiently. "I don't know so much about the code, but I know it's bad form for the first lieutenant of a ship to be fighting a duel with one of the other officers. However, if you think that's what I ought to do, Dr. Lining, go to Mr. Lee and tell him that I think it is a breach of the proprieties to fight aboard the ship, but if McNulty insists on it I'll accommodate him. You and Mr. Lee can arrange time, place, and weapons."

"You know, Smith," said Lining to Lee, "that Whittle is not afraid to fight McNulty, but it would be a bad example to the men for the chief officer to fight a duel on board. How could he ever punish one of them for fighting if he set such an example? Furthermore, there's no suitable place on board for a duel with pistols. I assume, of course, that you agree with me that gentlemen couldn't settle their differences by fisticuffs."

Lee readily agreed to this lofty principle, but suggested that a pistol duel might be staged on the poop deck. Lining objected that such a public place was out of the question.

"How could a gentleman be expected to settle an affair of honor in the presence of the officer of the deck, the quartermaster, and the man at the wheel? A duel is essentially a private affair. The poop deck would never do."

"How about the wardroom?" asked Lee, who was unwilling to see the plans for the duel fall through.

"Oh, great heavens, no!" exclaimed Lining. "That would be entirely too dangerous to the rest of us at such close quarters if either of them should miss. And you must bear in mind, if any unfortunate accident should occur, we seconds could be charged with murder when we get to port. Duelling is murder under the English law."

This put an entirely different complexion on the matter, and Lee's enthusiasm for the combat began to wane. Perhaps he had better see Dr. McNulty again, he said. He came back with the report that McNulty had agreed to a postponement of the affray, but insisted that he must have satisfaction as soon as they reached port. To this Lining agreed, on Whittle's behalf, and so the blood-letting was averted.

Although the duel was not fought, its discussion and the attendant agitation served to widen still further the breach between the two factions among the officers. McNulty got drunk again and had a bloody fight with O'Brien in the steerage. Manning and Blacker came to blows over a trifling dispute. McGuffeny took Manning's part and threatened Blacker; then when Hunt upheld Blacker, McGuffeny offered to whip them both, singly or together, which generous offer was not accepted.

Discipline was crumbling as the fugitive ship plunged on along her northward course. The captain was alternately lax and stern, buoyant and moody. Things would run along at loose ends for a week or so, and then he would suddenly issue some arbitrary restrictive order. "No sitting on the weather side of the quarter-deck," or, "Men must not sit on the rail."

"Why?" asked the men.

"Because the skipper says so," was all the explanation they got. The men grew increasingly resentful. Below decks the quarreling and fighting continued intermittently. In the wardroom the officers exchanged sharp words or sat in sullen silence.

"It's a perfect hell afloat!" Dr. Lining exclaimed bitterly as he returned from one of his frequent professional visits to the steerage. "Hell afloat!"

CHAPTER NINETEEN

HOME IS THE SAILOR

═════════

Contrary to the dire apprehensions expressed by the nervous officers after they had rounded the Horn, no storms were encountered by the Shenandoah as she made her way through the North Atlantic during the early days of November. Only moderate winds blew, no more ominous-looking vessels appeared, and Captain Waddell felt justified in beginning to make arrangements for a final disposition of the ship's affairs once she reached Liverpool.

The first matter on his mind was the payment of the crew. The Southern Confederacy was a thing of the past, but he felt that his first obligation was to see that these men who had carried the Stars and Bars around the world should receive their promised pay, at least so far as it was within his power to give it to them.

Calling Lieutenant Whittle and Paymaster Smith into his cabin, he threshed out the matter with them as the ship forged ahead, drawing closer and closer to Liverpool.

"The men must be paid," he decreed firmly. "Without them the expedition would have been im-

274

possible. They've earned their pay, and they'll need it when they're set ashore. But unfortunately," he went on, "our sailing fund has been very sadly depleted by the repairs and other expenses at Melbourne. We spent upwards of $18,000 there, and that leaves only a little more than $4,000 of the original fund of $22,000—not nearly enough to pay off the men for all the time they've served. There's only one thing to do about it in my opinion, Mr. Smith. Figure up what each man will have coming to him when we reach Liverpool. We should be there by the sixth or seventh. Pay each his pro rata part of the $4,000 on hand, and give each of them a signed certificate for the unpaid balance. Then give me a list of the balance due, and I will turn it over to Mr. Bulloch in London and try to make arrangements with him to pay off the remainder if he has any Confederate funds left in his possession."

"Why not wait until we get there, and then pay them off?" Smith asked. "We could get from Mr. Bulloch what we need, put it with what we have, and then pay each man in full after we land."

"No, that won't do," objected Waddell. "I plan to surrender the ship to the British government the minute we get there, and if we had any of the sailing fund in the safe the Yankees would naturally try to seize it. If we divide it up out here today, the men will have it in their pockets, and it won't be subject to seizure."

"What about the money we've taken off the prizes?" Smith inquired. "You know, you've had me keep that separate and apart from the sailing fund.

Shall I divide the prize money among the men too? There's not much of it. It amounts to—let me see." He looked at his books. "It amounts to $820.40."

"I've been thinking about that," Waddell said. "Maybe it's Quixotic, but, to my way of thinking, that money falls in a different category from when we started out. The sailing money was ours to begin with and is still ours. The men must have it. But that little dab of money we took off the prizes is just funds we are holding in trust. It doesn't belong to us. To use it for paying off the men would be little short of embezzlement. It must be surrendered with the ship."

"Aren't you bending backward?" Whittle asked. "Why should we be so careful about the Yankees' money? The men we took it from will never get it back anyhow. Why not give it to our men? They'll need all they can get, set down in a strange port."

But Captain Waddell refused to argue the matter. "No," he said, "I've been thinking about it for days, and my mind is made up. I can't see it any other way. Divide up the sailing fund with the men, Mr. Smith, but keep the prize money intact to be surrendered. It's the only honorable thing to do."

On November 4 the reckoning of position showed them to be near the land, and all hands on deck, as well as the lookouts aloft, eagerly scanned the horizon for a first glimpse of the British coast. Night fell, however, with no land yet in sight, and when the following morning came, a dense fog obscured everything at a ship's length. The vessel now proceeded with the most extreme caution. There were only the chronometers and the patent log to rely on for computing the position, and the chronometers had of necessity gone so long unchecked that there was some doubt of their accuracy. But there was nothing that could be done about that now, so with all sails furled and with the constant blast of the whistle raising muffled echoes in the fog, she steamed slowly ahead, the firemen's scoops scraping the bottom of the bunkers as they shoveled in the last few tons of the dwindling supply of fuel.

At length, like the rolling up of a curtain, the fleecy fog lifted. An involuntary cheer rose from the deck as the disappearing mist revealed off the port bow the welcome sight of rolling green land, the first land they had laid their eyes on since they had dashed through the Aleutian Islands chain.

"Ireland, by all that's holy!" exclaimed Matt O'Brien, and Ireland it was.

The sight of the land was a tonic for the men. Forgotten now was their privation, their hardship, their thirst, and their fears. Even the men in the sick bay, worn down by the ravages of scurvy smiled when the glad news was brought below.

Land! Nobody knew what troubles might lie ahead of them, but the deck was crowded with happy, haggard faces as the vessel glided on toward Tuska Rock Light. Soon the light was abeam, and they were steaming on to the northward and eastward toward Holyhead on the last lap of their voyage.

Captain Waddell could hardly contain himself as the ship made her way up St. George's Channel, all the perils of the deep behind her, no matter what perils lay ahead. Calling Bulloch to his cabin, he congratulated him. Bulloch was one of those who had signed the offending letter, but he had showed himself to be a mariner of the first class, and this was a time to let bygones be bygones.

"A splendid piece of navigating, Mr. Bulloch," the captain greeted him warmly. "In all my years on the sea I've never seen a better landfall. And it's all the more creditable when I think of the difficulties you have experienced. Not a chance to rate the chronometers since leaving Melbourne. Not a sight of land in 23,000 miles. And then the beacon in St. George's showed up just where it was looked for! Your navigating is very beautiful, Mr. Bulloch."

Young Bulloch flushed with pleasure at this warm praise from the skipper.

"I hope, sir," he stammered, "that you'll not hold that letter against me. I—"

"Forget it, my boy, forget it. It was just a case of youthful nervousness, I reckon. But there's nothing youthful about your navigating. I'll tell the whole world that you're a born sailor."

It was after midnight when the pilot's boat was seen bobbing down the channel, and as the pilot came over the side he was greeted by Lieutenant Whittle with a cheery "Good morning."

"Good morning," returned the pilot. "What ship is this?"

"The late Confederate steamer Shenandoah," replied Mr. Whittle, with just a faint note of pride in his voice.

"The hell it is!" exclaimed the pilot. "The Shen-

278

andoah? Why I was reading but a few days ago of your being in the Arctic Ocean."

"Well, that's where we've come from," replied Whittle.

"Haven't you stopped at any port since you left there?"

"No, nor been in sight of land either. But tell me, what's the latest news about the war in America?"

"The war?" repeated the pilot, as though trying to recall some dim episode of ancient history. "Why, the war's been over so long people have stopped talking about it. The Southern armies have all surrendered long ago, and Jeff Davis is locked up in Fort Monroe. The Yankees have had a lot of cruisers out looking for you. They'll be wild when they find out you've outwitted them."

The pilot was so much excited over the arrival of the cruiser that he ran her aground in trying to cross the bar. There she was forced to remain while the whole ship's company fumed in impatience until the rising tide freed her the following morning. Shortly after sun-up the steamer was clear of the bar, and slowly and proudly she steamed up the Mersey toward the city, with the Confederate ensign flying from her masthead. It was just a ghost of a flag now, but it was the only flag to which they had any claim, and Captain Waddell was determined, as a matter of pride and sentiment, to carry his colors to the bitter end. During the afternoon she reached the ship's basin. At Captain Waddell's order, the pilot brought her up astern of Her Majesty's ship of the line, Donegal, where she was anchored.

As the cruiser's anchors splashed into the Mersey's muddy tide and the vessel's forward progress stopped, Lieutenant Whittle stood on the poop, his arms folded. He had one last duty to perform—the saddest duty of all. Slowly he raised his right hand above his head, then quickly lowered it. In response to the signal, the quartermaster tugged at the halyards, and the flag came fluttering down to the deck, slowly and haltingly as though conscious of the tragic futility of the event.

"It's hard to think—" the young lieutenant began to Captain Waddell, who had come up and stood silently by his side. Something in his throat made it impossible for him to go on.

The captain put his hand on his shoulder, kindly and comfortingly. "I know."

The quartermaster on the deck was folding up the piece of bunting. As he finished that funereal task, Mr. Whittle brushed his hand quickly across his eyes, and, turning quickly, walked off to his cabin.

CHAPTER TWENTY

AFTER THE END

CAPTAIN PAYNTER of the Donegal, aroused from his afternoon nap, accepted the surrender of the Shenandoah with characteristic British calm, as though receiving errant Confederate cruisers were an ordinary event in his life. Putting on his dress uniform, he called for his gig and was rowed to the wanderer's side.

As soon as the Britisher came on board, Captain Waddell handed to him a letter which he had sat up late the night before to write. It was addressed to Earl Russell, announcing his arrival in the waters of the Mersey and his desire to surrender to the British government. Briefly he mentioned the singular position in which he had found himself placed as a result of "having engaged in acts of war as late as the 28th of June, in ignorance of the obliteration of the government under whose authority I was acting." He told of receiving the news of the war's end from the Barracouta.

"I was in an embarrassing position. I diligently examined all the law writers at my command, searching for a precedent for my guidance in the future control, management, and final disposal of the vessel. I could find none. History is, I believe, without a parallel. Finding the authority questionable under which I could consider this vessel a ship of war, I immediately discontinued cruising and shaped my course for the Atlantic ocean. As to the ship's disposal, I do not consider that I have any right to destroy her or any further right to command her. On the contrary, I think that as all the property of the Confederate government has reverted by the fortune of war to the government of the United States, that therefore this vessel, insofar as it was the property of the Confederate States, should accompany the other property already reverted. I have therefore sought this port as a suitable one to learn the news; and, if I am without a government, to surrender the ship, with her battery, small arms, machinery, stores, tackle and apparel complete, to Her Majesty's government, for such disposition as in its wisdom it shall deem proper."

This letter was duly forwarded to Earl Russell. Awaiting the decision of the diplomats, the gunboat Goshawk was brought up and lashed alongside the Shenandoah and a prize crew of fifty armed sailors and marines put aboard under the command of Lieutenant Cheek, along with the necessary customs officers.

"You understand," Lieutenant Cheek announced to the Shenandoah's assembled officers in his sternest and most formal Brittanic manner, "that you will be held as prisoners until Her Majesty's pleasure regarding you is known. Also, you will understand, you will not be permitted to take the vessel out of the port again without permission."

"Take her out again?" said Lee to Whittle with a grin. "Isn't that a thick-headed limey for you? Why would we want to take her out when we've just sailed 20,000 miles, halfway around the world, to bring her in? Where do you suppose he thinks we'd go?"

As soon as the news of the cruiser's arrival was heard on shore, there was great excitement among the Confederate sympathizers in Liverpool. Captain Whitehead, of the firm of Whittaker, Whitehead & Company, showed himself a thoughtful Samaritan by promptly sending out a boatload of food supplies, the very thing the men on board so sorely needed. There were fresh beef and mutton, vegetables, eggs and cheese, two or three tubs of butter, and plenty of fresh bread, not to mention two barrels of ale and one of porter. The half-famished crew had their first square meal for many weeks, and the scurvy-ridden invalids in the sick bay began to feel better immediately. The next day a similar boatload of fresh foodstuffs was sent out by another friendly Englishman, but by that time the stern Lieutenant Cheek was in charge, and the boat was not permitted to discharge its precious cargo. "We'll feed our prisoners." Cheek announced crisply, as the hungry men with sad eyes watched the boatload of provisions go back to the shore.

Meanwhile the arrival of the Shenandoah had thrown Anglo-American diplomatic affairs into a turmoil. As soon as the cruiser was seen in the Mersey, the consul at Liverpool had telegraphed Adams at London, who hurried to call on Lord Clarendon at the foreign office. Lord Clarendon had also just heard the news, and though inclined to be incredulous, discussed the matter informally with Adams.

Adams, in a letter to Secretary Seward, admitted frankly that, confronted with this unusual situation, he was not quite sure what to do. "The character in which the Shenandoah may be viewed," he wrote, "by the British government as well as by ourselves, being two-fold, I endeavored to avoid the necessity of defining it. If I had made the claim to the vessel on the score of its having been a Confederate, it would have appeared virtually to recognize the justice of the recognition of it heretofore by the British government. If I had demanded it as a pirate, preying upon our commerce, the answer might be that it was in that capacity amenable to the laws of Great Britain, and might therefore be retained here, subject to the ordinary process of forfeiture in the courts. My object has been to make the demand in such a shape as to throw the responsibility of the designation of the cause of delivery entirely upon the British government, without committing us to it in any manner. So also with the men. I foresaw that if I claimed them as pirates under the extradition treaty, the answer that I should get would be a call for proof before the courts. If I claimed them as prisoners, the reply would be still more prompt and conclusive, the war being admitted to be entirely at an end."

The London *Times* on November 8 carried a ponderous and pointedly unfriendly editorial on the subject of the problem. "The reappearance of the Shen-

andoah in British waters at the present juncture," it
stated inhospitably in its opening sentence, "is an
untoward and unwelcome event." It reviewed the
cruiser's career, making the callous suggestion that
"it would have been a great relief to us, though
little to the advantage of the United States, had the
Shenandoah been simply excluded from the Mersey
and left to rove the seas till she should fall into the
hands of her pursuers." The editorial closed by admitting that the Shenandoah's personnel could not
be taken as prisoners of war, and suggesting that
they be prosecuted for piracy.

While the "thunderer" belched forth its hostile
comments and Adams and Lord Clarendon engaged
in their skillful verbal fencing, the men on board the
Shenandoah were growing restless and resentful
under their detention. On the morning of the seventh
the crew demanded of Lieutenant Cheek that they be
permitted to land, but he was able to persuade them
to remain quiet for a day or two until orders could be
obtained from London. On the morning of the eighth
Cheek became alarmed over the possibility of dis-
order and wrote to Captain Paynter, "The men are
getting riotous and determined to stay on board no
longer—eight or ten have already deserted." He
continued that he had heard that one or two of the
officers had said that they were going to leave that
evening at all risks, and he urged that something be
done promptly to relieve the tense state of affairs, as
he doubted his ability to keep the men under control.

Fortunately the Foreign Office announced its decision that day. The Shenandoah, Lord Clarendon

proclaimed, should be immediately turned over to the representatives of the United States, along with all its stores and fittings. The officers, he announced, should be released, as there was no charge that could be made and sustained against them. As for the crew, he said, all of them who were not British subjects should also be released. If there were any British subjects on board, they should be detained and prosecuted under the terms of the foreign enlistment act.

On the evening of the eighth Captain Paynter arrived on board with the news of Lord Clarendon's decision. The men were hastily mustered on deck, and Lieutenant Whittle prepared to call out their names from the muster-roll.

"As your name is called," said Paynter to the men, "you will answer and give the place of your birth." The news had already spread by grapevine throughout the ship's company that it would not be healthy to admit being a Britisher, and that a declaration of Southern birth insured a clean bill of health. So, as their names were called they gravely stepped forward —Englishmen, Irishmen, Scots, and Norwegians— and declared themselves to be natives of Virginia, Louisiana, or whatever Southern state's name came into their minds. When the roll call was over, as was meet and proper on a Confederate cruiser, every man Jack aboard was a native of the South. They were all sent trooping ashore.

This disposition of the matter, however, was by no means pleasing to the authorities of the United States. Seward almost exploded when he heard the

news and wrote protestingly to Adams that he should
have demanded the surrender of every man on board
the ship as fugitives from justice and brought them
to America where they could be "punished for their
flagrant crimes."

Captain Paynter came in for his share of criticism
too. It should have been obvious, said his critics, that
all those sailors were not native Southerners. Paynter, they strongly hinted, had knowingly connived at
the defeat of justice. Rankling under these attacks,
Paynter made a formal answer and defense of his
conduct in which, with a fine display of ruffled dignity, he said, "I trust I may be pardoned if, as a
British officer accustomed during my whole period of
service to the uniform and cleanly appearance of
British man-of-war's men, I could not pronounce on
my own responsibility whether some of the dirty,
drawling, gray-coated, big-bearded men who passed
before me as the crew of the Shenandoah were British
subjects or American citizens."

The British newspapers engaged in a lively controversy about the matter, some on one side and
some on the other. In a letter to the London *Stand-
ard*, Sir James Elphistone pointed out that Captain
Waddell's activities after the official cessation of
hostilities were not entirely without precedent, men-
tioning the case of the American man-of-war Hornet
which on March 23, 1815, destroyed the British
sloop of war Penguin, several months after the signing of the Treaty of Ghent. This added new fuel to
the flames of the controversy, and its reverberations
extended even to the newspapers of Australia.

Meanwhile the Shenandoah's officers and men were busy ashore winding up their affairs. Captain Waddell, along with most of the other officers, went to the Waterloo Hotel in Liverpool where he immediately communicated with Bulloch. The men of the crew were instructed to put up at the Sailors' Home, where they were to wait until arrangements could be made to pay them off. Bulloch, fortunately, still had Confederate funds on hand, and he provided the necessary money to pay off the wages still due the men. The assistant paymaster appeared at the Sailors' Home on the morning of the eleventh and started the welcome task of exchanging British pounds and shillings for the certificates of unpaid balances. Gold was also forthcoming to pay off the amounts due the officers. There was later some mutter that the assistant paymaster did not pay out all the money entrusted to him, and it was charged that he fled to London in disguise and was never seen again. But most of the men seemed to be well satisfied to be back in England alive, and if there was any actual defalcation, there was surprisingly little complaint about it.

Captain Waddell, at last relieved of the trying responsibilities of his duties, reacted by bursting a blood vessel and became an invalid at his hotel for several months. The other officers were somewhat at a loss what to do, having been notified that they had been specifically excluded from the terms of the post-war general amnesty and that it would not be safe for them to return to the United States. Lieutenant

Whittle, accompanied by Lee, Mason, and Browne, left Liverpool in December and went to Buenos Aires, South America at that time being a popular place of refuge for expatriated Confederates. After prospecting for a while they went to Rosario on the Rio Parana, and near there bought a small place and went to farming. When they thought it safe, Browne and Mason returned to the States, and still later Whittle and Lee came home. Dr. Lining also succumbed to the South American lure. He went to Brazil and lived there until the ban was lifted in 1875. Grimball and some of the others went to Mexico, and one or two of them stayed in England.

Captain Waddell remained in England until 1875, but in September of that year he returned to the United States and was promptly engaged by the Pacific Mail Line as a merchant captain to take charge of its newest liner, the San Francisco, just built to ply the Pacific between Australia and California. Waddell took the new ship, a 4,000-ton steamer, from New York to Melbourne, where he was greeted with an ovation.

Here she took on passengers and cargo for her maiden trip to San Francisco, but she never arrived at her destination. Off the coast of Mexico, running along in a smooth sea and under a cloudless sky, the new steamer went aground on a rock unmarked on any of the charts. Although no lives were lost, Captain Waddell suffered the humiliation of losing his first peacetime command. The company, however, exonerated him of all blame, and he remained in their service as a commander. An ironical fact in con-

nection with the disaster to the San Francisco was
that the rock on which she struck had been discovered by a government vessel in 1863 and duly reported to the Navy Department. Secretary Welles,
however, was so busy at that time with the prosecu-
tion of the war that the report had been pigeon-
holed and forgotten, and the location of the rock
remained unmarked on the charts.

After several years' service with the Pacific Mail,
Waddell resigned and, despite his years, took active
charge of the fight being carried on by the state of
Maryland against the oyster pirates in Chesapeake
Bay. This was an anticlimactic end for a world-
roving Rebel raider, but the oyster pirates were
vigorously attacked and effectively suppressed. Waddell died March 15, 1886.

The Shenandoah herself was formally turned over
to the United States authorities on November 11,
1865, and on that day an American officer, Captain
Thomas F. Freeman, and a skeleton crew were put
on board. The British washed their hands of the
matter. As soon as he could get a full crew together,
Freeman started out to sail the vessel to New York,
but within a few days the prudent captain was back
in Liverpool. The ship, he reported, was too frail to
combat the storms and heavy seas of the North Atlantic, and he had deemed it unsafe to continue the
voyage.

The Shenandoah then lay in the Liverpool docks
for months, a sort of nautical white elephant, but at
length she was sold to the Sultan of Zanzibar for his
use as a private royal yacht, and he rechristened her

the Majidi. The Sultan's entire fleet, including the Majidi, was wrecked by a hurricane which swept Zanzibar in April, 1872. Soon afterward a British salvage ship pulled her off the sand beach where she was aground, and she was patched up enough to be able to run to Bombay with the fair monsoon to be docked and repaired. In July of 1872 she set out from Bombay for Zanzibar in charge of a German captain and a native crew, but she never reached her destination. Soon after a British warship, the Briton, cruising in the Mozambique Channel, picked up a boat containing the sole survivors, who stated that the Majidi, or Shenandoah, had been scuttled. "This," reported the commander of the Briton, without revealing the basis for his suspicion, "was probably the work of the Germans, who wanted the Sultan to buy a ship from Hamburg. So ends the history of the Shenandoah."

BIBLIOGRAPHY

Official Records of the Union and Confederate Navies, Series 1, Volume 3. Washington, 1896.

Claims of U. S. Against Great Britain, Volume III; First Session 41st Congress, 1869. ("Correspondence Concerning Claims Against Great Britian, Transmitted to the Senate of the U. S.")

The Case of the United States to be Laid Before the Tribunal of Arbitration to be Convened at Geneva. Washington, 1872.

History of the Confederate States Navy, J. F. Scharff. New York, 1887.

The Cruise of the Shenandoah, Cornelius E. Hunt. New York, 1867.

Southern Historical Society Papers. Richmond, Va.

The Confederate Veteran. Nashville, Tenn.